The Collecto

SKI-DOO
Snowmobiles

Philip J. Mickelson

Enthusiast Books
1830A Hanley Road
Hudson, Wisconsin 54016 USA

www.enthusiastbooks.com

© 2004 Philip J. Mickelson

Library of Congress Control Number: 2004109096

ISBN-10: 1-58388-133-6
ISBN-13: 978-1-58388-133-0

Reprinted November 2013

Printed in The United States of America

On the front cover: A classic 1960 Ski-Doo (serial number 190) shares the snow with a 1994 Ski-Doo Summit 670. *Lance Parthe*

BOOK PROPOSALS

Enthusiast Books is a publishing company specializing in books for transportation enthusiasts. We publish in a number of different areas, including Automobiles, Auto Racing, Buses, Construction Equipment, Emergency Equipment, Farming Equipment, Railroads & Trucks. The Enthusiast Books imprint is constantly growing and expanding into new subject areas.

Authors, editors, and knowledgeable enthusiasts in the field of transportation history are invited to contact the Editorial Department at Enthusiast Books, 1830A Hanley Road, Hudson, WI 54016.

Contents

Acknowledgments

Thank you to all the Bombardier employees, dealers, and Ski-Doo® enthusiasts who helped me assemble the stories and history of the machine that changed winter... Ski-Doo.

A special thanks to France Bissonnette, directrice, J. Armand Bombardier Museum, and Carl Eisan, curator, J. Armand Bombardier Museum, for letting me dig through the archives in the museum and allowing the use of many rare photographs from the museum.

One of the wonderful people I met while researching the book was Omer Nadeau. Mr. Nadeau worked with J. Armand Bombardier during his development of the Ski-Doo and didn't stop working for the company for fifty years! Thank you for the insight you gave me into those early years and for the numerous details you filled in for me regarding the development of the very first Ski-Doos.

My own history with Ski-Doo started while working with Tom Halvorson, who had founded Halvorson Equipment Company with his father to distribute Bombardier tractors in the Midwest years before Ski-Doo came along. Halvorson's distributorship grew rapidly with the advent of Ski-Doo and he was an instrumental part of Ski-Doo's rapid growth in popularity in the United States. The 1960 Ski-Doo pictured on the cover is the first one sold by Halvorson Equipment. Tom supplied me with many of the original communications between Bombardier Ltd. and their distributors as well as numerous brochures from the early years. The specifications and details of Ski-Doo's growth could not have been nearly as complete without your help, Tom. Thank you!

Thanks to the Ehlert Publishing Group for letting me dig through your photo files. Thirty years of publishing snowmobile magazines has left you with an historical treasure!

Gerard Karpik is, himself, part of Ski-Doo's history. Thanks for supplying several critical photos and lots of detail information, Gerard.

I pestered many Bombardier employees for details of numerous models. A special thanks to Sam LaPointe, Jean-Paul Samson, Gilles LeVesque, Henry Wilson, and Gordy Radtke.

Dave Mahler has a personal history with Ski-Doo that dates almost to the beginning. Thanks for the help with the names and details, Dave.

Perhaps the premiere restorer and collector of significant Ski-Doo models is Bill Fullerton. I appreciate the help and trouble you went to in supplying photos of your beautifully restored Ski-Doos, Bill.

Thanks, too, to the boys at Minnesota Outdoor Recreation in Duluth, Minnesota, for letting me drag every parts book and many service manuals out of the shop. That information was invaluable in verifying many of the subtle changes that occurred over the years.

Preface

Since I was born and raised in Duluth, Minnesota, one would think I would have enjoyed winter, you know, skiing, skating, hockey. No, I am a machine kind of person. Motorcycles were my passion and winter simply forced me into the basement to work on bikes, that is, when I wasn't shoveling the latest downfall. When I was out of school, I had looked forward to moving to warmer climes and enjoying my passion year round.

A phone call from Halvorson Equipment Company, distributors for Ski-Doo, caught my attention when they said they were expanding their racing program. I didn't know much about snowmobiles but I knew engines and these guys wanted to pay me to build racing engines. I was dropped into the world of snowmobile racing with greats like Steve Ave, George and sons Stan and Doug Hayes, Gary Scott, Yvon DuHammel, and Bob Fortin. I learned about snowmobiles in a hurry!

Ski-Doo and the winter of 1968-1969 changed how I felt about winter. The long hours spent modifying Ski-Doos was fun... testing and riding Ski-Doos was great... racing Ski-Doos was absolutely fantastic! That was the first winter I remembered as *fun*.

There were a few snow-going machines crawling around the snowbelt before the first Ski-Doo but one would have a hard time defining them as what we call snowmobiles. All one has to do is compare a 1959 Ski-Doo to any of them to see why Joseph-Armand Bombardier has been called the inventor of the snowmobile. His little Ski-Doo changed winter for millions of us who now can't wait for the first snowfall.

Phil Mickelson
Duluth, Minnesota

Chapter 1

The Beginning, 1959-1965

Joseph-Armand Bombardier devoted his entire life to looking for mechanical designs that would conquer the elements in his part of the world. In Valcourt, Quebec, Canada, that meant about five months of often incredibly deep snow. As a talented, young mechanic, Bombardier opened a garage in Valcourt in 1926. He made his living repairing tractors and automobiles but for nearly a decade he tinkered with various single and two-passenger snowmobile designs. Had he continued working on the smaller machines, the Ski-Doo as we came to know it may have evolved earlier.

In January of 1934, Armand and his wife Yvonne's 2-year old son developed acute appendicitis. The nearest hospital was a little over 20 miles (mi) away and all roads were snowed in. An unfinished snowmobile sat in Armand's garage as his young son passed away, unable to get to medical treatment and inaccessible to doctors who might have treated him. The tragic loss of his son helped focus Armand on finding a solution to the winter isolation of the snow belt. He redirected his efforts, setting aside the one- and two-passenger machine in favor of designs that could transport several passengers. The Ski-Doo would have to wait!

Bombardier developed his rubber-covered drive sprocket design in 1935, leading to his development of many successful track drive systems and to his financial success. The sprocket was so instrumental in the success of his vehicles, it would become part of the Bombardier Snowmobile logo and is still seen in Bombardier, Inc.'s logo.

Bombardier developed and produced many different designs between 1935 and 1958, all track-driven and designed for use in soft terrain and snow, but all were quite large vehicles.

Bombardier had a friend working as a missionary in Northern Ontario, Father Maurice Ouimet. He wrote this letter to Ouimet on March 15, 1956:

"I have just received a letter from Father Dorge, who includes a clipping from the Winnipeg *Free Press* of last 6 March which wrote about the success our Muskeg tractors have had in his territory. I am willing to admit that these vehicles may be a little pricy and that they may be of limited practical use for most of your missionaries.

"Following the entreaties of several missionaries, including Father Dorge, I think we might still be able to come up with a small vehicle with a light motor and with a single track that would be as wide as the vehicle itself."

Reading the letter, one can almost feel the wheels turning in Bombardier's head. The short note almost spells out the design that is in his mind. Bombardier didn't dive into the

Bombardier tried two skis on this twin-track prototype but lost traction with the design. *J-A Bombardier Museum*

small machine project for another year but his oldest son, Germain, was working on a seamless, wide track for a ski trail grooming machine that would spur the final design of what would become the original Ski-Doo. In 1957, Bombardier tested one of the original concepts on the Salmon River in Kingsbury, Quebec. The design utilized several of Germain's concepts, including a chaincase connecting the output of the transmission to the axle driving the seamless, full-width track. The machine was the smallest and lightest that Bombardier had tested since he put away the smaller machines in 1934 but it was still a much larger machine than he had in mind. Armand worked through 1957 and 1958, coming up with a wood-bodied prototype incorporating two 15 inch (in) wide tracks and twin skis. The machine utilized a Kohler en-

gine with a vertical crankshaft that connected through a centrifugal clutch to the gear box driving twin drive axles. It was very much lighter than the model tested in Kingsbury and showed some real promise!

In testing with the machine, it was discovered that the twin tracks, when used with the two-ski design, would lose traction in uneven terrain. With a ski at both corners, high surfaces would push up on the ski, lifting a portion of one track off the surface. A second version was built using one ski in the middle along with twin 15in-wide tracks. This design worked better than the twin ski arrangement but turned more slowly and was still a larger machine than Armand was interested in.

1959

The wood components of the original machine were duplicated in shape and function in steel, and twenty-five all metal Ski-Dogs were built in the winter of 1958-1959. These twenty-five original machines were equipped with a two-speed, planetary gear box mounted on the top of the chaincase. With the engine started, pulling back on the control lever selected low gear. Increasing the engine rpm engaged the drive line and you were off. Letting go of the control lever allowed the planetary system to run in high gear. Bombardier quickly replaced the planetary drive system with variable diameter drive and driven pulleys. (Only one of the twenty-five original machines is known to have survived with the original transmission. It is on display in the J-Armand Bombardier Museum in Valcourt, Quebec.)

These machines had no lights or backrests and the seat cushion was divided in two parts to allow a tube to pass over the tunnel that reinforced the foot rests. The original twenty-five machines had no windshield and the hood only had the name "Bombardier" written in script on it.

A single-ski version of the sled worked better and taught Bombardier lessons that would be remembered on the first twin-track Ski-Doo. *J-A Bombardier Museum*

Armand, Germain, and their workers built three prototype versions of light machines in 1958. One of them incorporated a single 15in-wide track with two skis set wider apart than the width of the track. Armand seemed satisfied with the wood prototype of what was then being referred to, in house, as the "Ski-Dog."

The plywood-hooded prototype of the original Ski-Doo. *J-A Bombardier Museum*

J-Armand is shown testing his prototype "Ski-Dog". *J-A Bombardier Museum*

This early photo shows the planetary gear box with control lever at the top of the chaincase on one of the original Ski-Doos built in the winter of 1958-1959. *J-A Bombardier Museum*

1960 ★★★★★	SK-60

Mass production if the Ski-Dog began with a run of 229 machines for the fall of 1959. Somewhere during that original production run, the name of the little snowmobile was changed from Ski-Dog to Ski-Doo. There are two stories about how the name change actually happened. Pick the one you like the best, for however it actually happened, the nearly accidental change created a name that became the most recognized in snowmobiling.

One story suggests that a typographical error was made on some printed materials being prepared for a Bombardier sales convention and "Dog" became "Doo." Armand was shown the error and he liked it. It was a name that read well in French and in English and it was "catchy." The little machine had a new name.

A second story suggests that when the actual mass production of the little machine

"Bombardier"

...years ago, BOMBARDIER stepped out of beaten paths to manufacture revolutionary off-road vehicles and NOW, proudly presents its actual line of vehicles.

Organizations all over the world rely upon this well known name to solve transportation problems in snow, muskeg, soft soil, mountainous and rough terrain.

Travel in comfort in a 12 passenger snowmobile equipped with a 6 cylinder engine or in a 15 passenger with a V-8 engine.

Muskeg tractor: the most versatile all-purpose vehicle with a long record of achievements in the field of oil and mineral exploration, public utilities and services, etc.

SKIDOG: the motorized dog team

J-5 tractor: the compact, powerful and reliable tractor whose applications and uses are unlimited.

This brochure from August, 1959, still refers to the sled as "Ski Dog," yet the hood of the machine clearly shows the triangular "Ski-Doo" logo. *Tom Halvorson*

started, the worker who was making the stencil to be used to paint the logo on the hood of the machine was having a devil of a time working the tail of the "g" into the triangular logo that was to be used. He finally gave up and left the tail off, effectively changing the name to Ski-Doo. The change was shown to Armand who, as in story one, liked the name and approved its use.

A letter dated August 10, 1959, from Alphonse-Raymond Bombardier, Armand's brother and sales manager for Bombardier Snowmobile Limited, introduced a new piece of literature to their dealers. Alphonse's cover letter noted: ."..Some units such as the ...and the SKI DOO are not freely offered yet due to difficulties in obtaining the engines. ..." He used the name, 'SKI DOO' but spelled it without using a hyphen. The brochure mailed with the letter labeled the machine, "SKIDOG : the motorized dog team." The photo of the machine on the brochure clearly showed the Bombardier name in script above the triangular shaped "SKI-DOO." The name change had clearly been made on the production machines but someone in the office wasn't aware of it and no one seemed too sure about how it should be written! No machine ever left the Bombardier factory with the name "Ski-Dog" on it.

Another letter from Alphonse-Raymond to their dealers, dated November 9, 1959, announced the arrival of Ski-Doo:

"Gentlemen:

"We are very happy to announce the arrival of our motorized snow-skooter: the SKIDOO.

"After two years of continuous trials, this vehicle is now ready for the production line and soon we will release a limited number.

"Once again, BOMBARDIER leads in bringing on the market and at a reasonable price, a vehicle which will facilitate transportation in remote and snowed in places. Also, it will be a most enjoyable sports item since it will be possible to make thrilling glides without getting puffed-out in climbing hills on foot.

"BOMBARDIER FIRST: This machine only weighs 335lb. and can be shoved in a standard automobile trunk.

"BOMBARDIER FIRST: Endless rubber belt practically covering the width of the vehicle and having no bolts nor fastened cross links.

"BOMBARDIER FIRST: A smooth and safe ride insured by series of rubbered wheels mounted on tandem and pressing against the inner surface of the rubber belt.

"BOMBARDIER FIRST: Automatic transmission with belt and sheaves allowing for easy operation even without experience and leaving the motor without drag for cold starting.

"Here are some classes of people which could benefit by motorising economically:

gendarmes (police, fish & game wardens), supervisors in forest operations and others, trappers, missionaries, explorers, prospectors, inspectors of power lines, micro-wave and tele-radio stations, etc., etc.

"MARKETING: We foresee a profitable business of those machines and urge you to order ONE IMMEDIATELY in order to familiarize yourselves with its operation and get acquainted with its qualities. The sharpness, the elegant and exclusive appearance of this SKIDOO will draw eager crowds at your demonstrations.

"We are listing here attached specifications, characteristics and prices.

"This is the season & time... let's SKIDOO

"Yours very truly,

"BOMBARDIER SNOWMOBILE LIMITED,

"Alp. Ray. Bombardier,

"Sales Manager.

"P.S. We hear that Santa sold his reindeers."

The translation of Alphonse's letter from French to English may not have been the best but his enthusiasm for the little Ski-Doo rang through loudly and clearly!

The original Ski-Doo had a suggested retail price of $990.00 (F.O.B. Valcourt) and was referred to as "Model SK-60." The machine was delivered with a twenty-five-page, French/English operator's manual that included a complete parts list, operating instructions, and maintenance procedures. An emergency tool kit and spare parts package were available for $22.00.

Bombardier's intent, when he focused his attention on the one- and two-passenger machine, was to build a light, inexpensive, maneuverable machine that could get those who *had* to travel over snow *over* it! As the Ski-Doo evolved it became very obvious to Armand and his staff that this little machine was just plain fun to operate. It is easy to understand Alphonse-Raymond's comment in his November 9, 1959 letter; "Also, it will make a most enjoyable sports item since it will be possible to make thrilling glides..." On the bottom of the first brochure introducing Ski-Doo to the Bombardier dealers was the company's slogan: "BOMBARDIER vehicles tread on hitherto untrodden ground."

Irv Benson, Saganaga Lake, Ontario, demonstrated a modern trapper's mode of transport in this 1960 Kohler engine ad. Irv still does a little trapping using a Ski-Doo Tundra but runs for groceries with his Ski-Doo Formula MX. *Kohler Co.*

Bombardier's Ski-Doo was about to tread on winter like it had never been tread upon before!

The original 225 production Ski-Doos were equipped with 5 foot (ft) long birch skis. The ski suspension consisted of coil springs that controlled a telescoping ski leg which attached with a pivoting bracket to the wooden ski. The bogie wheels in the track suspension were 8in in diameter and supported the top of the track as well as placing the weight of the machine on the track. The forward axle of the front tandem mounted three wheels while the back half of the tandem mounted two wheels. The rear tandem mounted two wheels on each axle. The rear axle mounted two sprockets with an 8in minor diameter. The throttle control was simply a choke cable affair mounted to the handlebar. While you could have referred to it as a very early cruise control, it wasn't the safest system with freezing snow and ice around. More than one Ski-Doo was known to have toured the country side riderless! A standard Kohler muffler was used and simply exited to the left side of the engine above the drive pulley assembly. It was noisy and, yes, the operator's left hand was always warmer than the right.

Probably all of the original 225 production Ski-Doos were built with no metal inserts covering the reinforcing rods and track between the sprocket holes on the inside of the track. A bulletin was issued on January 16, 1960, noting that, "An important improvement has been made to the track of the Ski-Doo... The reason for the change... is to prevent damage to the track due to the friction of rubber on rubber such as between track and sprocket." Metal inserts were provided to be installed on the machines that were in the field at the time of this development. A steel dolly was also provided to allow proper crimping of the inserts into the track when used with a hammer. This tool was used for many years as the approved manner for installing track clips during normal track maintenance.

The production models were all equipped with a bicycle headlight mounted on the hood

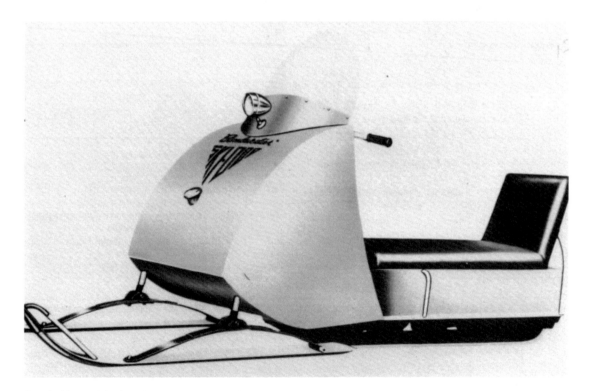

Steel skis and leaf springs were a vast improvement over the original birch skis with coil springs. *J-A Bombardier Museum*

The A-62 "Alpine" introduced shorter skis, a light, flexible bogie suspension system, and a reduction in weight of 85lb over the original Ski-Doo. *Lance Parthe*

and the taillight mounted on the back side of the hood at the upper left corner. Power was generated by a bicycle generator which had a rubber friction drive against the governor housing of the engine pulley.

Sales of the original 225 production Ski-Doos were going unexpectedly well when Alphonse-Raymond sent a letter to Bombardier dealers and distributors on January 4, 1960:

"Gentlemen:

"..we are very pleased to announce an important price reduction which will add to your sales potential. This reduction is possible by ...improving our equipment for production.

"It is understood that on your part you should refund immediately the difference between the previous suggested retail price of $990.00 and the new price of $866.00 that is an amount of $124.00 to each customer to whom you have sold or delivered a Ski-Doo."

In the same letter, Alphonse announced that the company would protect the Ski-Doos sold that first season with a ninety-day, parts-only warranty.

SK-60	
Dimensions	
Total length of body	72in
Total length with skis	106in
Width of body	30in
Total width with skis	33in
Height not including windshield	32in
Ski stance	27in
Weight and Performance	
Weight	335lb
Bearing surface	1,200sq in
Ground pressure	0.28lb/sq in
Maximum speed	25mph
Seating capacity	2
Approximate gas consumption	1/2gal/hr
Engine	
Make	Kohler, K-161P
Type	4-cycle, air-cooled, one cylinder
Horsepower	7hp at 3,600rpm
Drive	
Transmission	Roller chain in oil bath
	Automatic Belt & sheaves
Track and suspension	
Track	Endless (patented)
Width of track	15in
Length of track on ground	48in
Number of wheels	11
Sprocket gears (patented)	2
Wheels	Steel with rubber tires
Suspension	On tandems and springs
Throttle	Hand operated on steering handle
Miscellaneous	
Fuel tank capacity	4imp. gal
Crankcase capacity	1imp. qt SAE 10 to 30
Drive chain oil bath	1/2imp. qt SAE 30

1961	
★★★★	K-61
★★★★★	J-61

1961

Significant changes were made to the Ski-Doo for the 1961 model year. A letter to the dealers and distributors dated October 1, 1960, told of the improvements, which included:

"A. The muffler is now underneath the Ski-Doo in front of the track.

"B. The accelerator knob on the handle bar is now replaced by a lever which will be much easier to operate.

"C. The coil spring of the ski is replaced by a leaf spring.

"D. A new arrangement of motor support is now in use."

The 1961 Bombardier Ski-Doo was equipped with a 7hp Kohler engine, windshield, seat with backrest, and lights which

The first major race at Montreal in December 1961. Ski-Doo had a real advantage! *J-A Bombardier Museum*

were powered by the bicycle generator. The standard color was yellow! Suggested retail price was $765.00. The model number given the machine was K-61.

It appears that during the late summer of 1960, it was decided to equip some Ski-Doos, at an additional cost, with German-built JLO two-stroke cycle engines. These 247cc engines produced 8hp at 4000rpm and reduced the total weight of the machine by 10 pounds (lb). The JLO-equipped Ski-Doos were given the model number, J-61. The J-61 had a suggested retail price of $836.50 while the K-61 listed at $765.00. Adding a recoil starter to the J-61 added another $10.00 to the price. A recoil starter was not standard on the J-61 until mid-December of 1961. It is not known exactly what the split was between Kohler and JLO equipped machines in 1961 but total production for the model year was 729 units, more than tripling the original production run.

Because the JLO engines had a lighting coil in their magnetos, 12 volt (v) lighting sys-

tems were installed on machines equipped with JLO engines. Twelve volt head and taillights were used and an on/off switch was mounted on the dash area of the hood.

A bulletin to dealers dated December 8, 1960, announces the metal ski runner as "experimental."

"On the Ski-Doos you have received lately there may be some which are equipped with metal skis instead of wooden skis. These new skis are still in the experimental stage and are not standard equipment on the Ski-Doo.

"The complete metal ski is interchangeable with the wooden ski on the 1961 Ski-Doos ..."

It seems most 1961 models were produced with wooden skis but some late production models were produced with the steel ski blades. A November 15, 1961, bulletin notes: "Frequent inquiries are received regarding the possible change from wooden to metal skis and we give below details on this interchangeability."

Bombardier made conversion parts available to equip the earliest coil spring-suspended Ski-Doos with the leaf spring and steel ski blade. Because of this early and very practical conversion, not a lot of the original coil spring front ends exist today. A further improvement to the ski design was announced on February 9, 1961. The original leaf spring was fastened to the steel ski blade by two bolts welded to the ski blade. The spring had a slot at the front and a hole at the rear that fit over the welded bolts. The improved design utilized a pivot pin mount at the rear of the spring leaf. It was much sturdier and became the only replacement ski and leaf spring available. The new spring had a higher arch in it, offering more ski pressure for better turning and slightly more vertical travel of the ski.

1962	
★ ★ ★ ★ ★	A-62
★ ★ ★ ★	J-62
★ ★ ★ ★	K-62

1962

Armand was constantly looking for ways to reduce the weight of Ski-Doo, improve its performance in snow and increase its durability. The results of his weight reduction program became available on a 1962 model named the "Alpine." Model names had not been used on the Ski-Doo but Alphonse-Raymond's letter of December 11, 1961, seemed to signal a change:

"Gentlemen:

"We are pleased to announce that we are putting on the market a new BOMBARDIER Ski-Doo which will be identified by the name "ALPINE."

"A copy of the general specifications is included and we wish to draw your attention to the following advantages:

"A. The total weight of the Ski-Doo "ALPINE" is reduced to 250lb, which is a considerable advantage in soft snow as well as in handling it in a garage or in transportation.

"B. Its 6hp engine with recoil starter is easy to start and very economical although the speed of the Ski-Doo is reduced a few miles an hour.

"C. A new and very flexible suspension mechanism and additional wheels are used, allowing for a better contact of the track on the snow. With this new suspension, we obtain a better and longer service from the track.

"D. Lubrication of the "ALPINE" Ski-Doo is reduced to a minimum, leaving but two points to be lubricated regularly: the ski legs. The wheels and suspension parts are lubricated at three month intervals and the engine is lubricated by means of the oil mixed with the fuel.

"E. The total length of the "ALPINE" Ski-Doo is approximately one foot shorter than other models."

The name "ALPINE" was never put on the machine and I've never seen the name used in any literature as applying to a single-track model. The new lightweight Ski-Doo was simply given the model number "A-62." Suggested retail price for the new model was $693.75.

The A-62, like the other models for 1962, the Kohler powered K-62 and the JLO powered J-62, was built with all-steel construction. The skis were now steel and, like every production Ski-Doo to date, the hood/body/tunnel was a single-piece, all-steel design. The K-62 and the J-62 utilized the chassis of the previous season. The major change for these models was the use of shorter metal skis, which gave the machine an overall length of 93in, and the new fourteen-wheel suspension

It's a safe bet that none of the machines in that first race were equipped with the original throttle set-up. *Lance Parthe*

The "R" models used Rotax engines and fiber-glass hoods for the first time. *J-A Bombardier Museum*

system as designed initially for the new Alpine model. Probably because of its greater speed or its late production date, the J-62 received a brake. The A-62 and K-62 were not equipped with a brake. Other minor refinements were made to the K- and J-62s but the new little brother got most of the attention.

The steel chassis of the A-62 looked very much like the other Ski-Doos but while the standard cab had nearly vertical sides, the A-62's pitched in at the top toward the windshield. It was narrower at the top of the cab, saving material and weight, and provided a somewhat sleeker look. Measuring the top of the cab from corner to corner, one will find the A-62 to be 24 1/2in across while the J- and K-62s are 27 1/2in. The ski on the A-62 was the same new ski used on all the '62s and was narrower and shorter than what had been used on the previous Ski-Doos. The rest of the Alpine's chassis is nearly identical to those of the K-62 and J-62. The track suspension, which was used on all the '62s, incorporated three sets of four wheel tandems along with the rear axle to suspend the machine. The rubber wheels or bogies were only

5in in diameter, compared to the 8in wheels found on the other models. The new design gave the sled better traction, a softer ride, and considerably lighter weight. The design worked so well and was so trouble free that it exists almost unchanged to this day on the Élan model.

The A-62 and the J-62, because of their JLO engines with the lighting coil built in, were equipped with a 12v lighting system and an on/off switch mounted on the dash. The K-62 still used the bicycle generator driving off the pulley and the bicycle lights.

The A-62 was equipped with the smallest displacement, lowest horsepower engine ever used in a production model Ski-Doo. The 148cc, 6hp JLO engine provided a top speed of just over 20mph. Many production records of the early years of Ski-Doo were lost in a fire and the breakdown of production of each model for 1962 is not known. Total production of all three models for the year, however, was 2,103, nearly tripling the previous year's production.

A-62	
Dimensions	
Length of chassis	73 1/2in
Overall length (with skis)	93in
Width of chassis	30in
Overall width (with skis)	31 1/2in
Height without windshield	32in
Weight and Performance	
Weight	250lb
Bearing surface	1065sq in
Ground pressure	0.23lb/sq in
Maximum speed	22mph
Seating capacity	2
Approx. gas consumption	1/2gal/hr
Engine	
Type	JLO, 148cc, 2 cycle, 1 cyl
Horsepower	6hp at 4500rpm
Drive	Roller chain in oil bath
Transmission	Automatic; Belt and sheaves
Track and Suspension	
Track	Endless (patented)
Width of track	15 in
Length of track on ground	50 in
Number supporting wheels	14 (includes rear sprockets)
Drive sprockets (patented)	2
Wheels	Rubber
Suspension	On tandems and springs
Throttle	
Miscellaneous	
Fuel tank capacity	3 3/4 imp gals
Chaincase capacity	12 imp pt, SAE 30

	R	RD
Dimensions		
Length of chassis	73in	73in
Overall length (with ski)	93in	96 1/2in
Width of chassis	29in	35in
Height w/o windshield	34 3/4in	36 1/2in
Ski stance	23 1/4in	n/a
Track & Suspension		
Track	1, endless	2, endless
Width of track	15in	15in each
Length of track on ground	50in	50in
Number, supporting wheels	14, rubber	28, rubber
Drive sprockets	2	4
Suspension	Tandems and springs	Same
Drive	Roller chain in oil bath	Same
Transmission		
Automatic	Belt and sheaves	Same
Throttle	Hand operated on steering handle	
Brake	Hand operated on steering handle (R models only)	
Engine		
Type	1 cyl, 2 cycle, air cool	Same
Horsepower	Available 6-8hp	8hp
Displacement	163cc, 247cc	247cc
Weight & Performance		
Weight	230lb (6hp engine)	377lb
Bearing surface	1020sq-in	1804sq-in
Ground pressure	0.23lb/sq-in	.21lb/sq-in
Maximum speed	25mph (6hp)	22mph
Seating capacity	2	2
Approx. gas consumption	1/2gal/hr	1/2gal/hr
Miscellaneous		
Fuel capacity	3imp gal	6imp gal
Chain case capacity	1/2imp pt	1imp pt
Compartment under seat	None	33x15x6in
Tool compartment	In dash	In dash

Though it's been said that "the first snowmobile race was held the day the second machine was built", the first organized race to capture wide attention was held by the Montreal Commodore Club on the Back River in 1962. Forty entrants participated in the event and it wasn't long before Bombardier discovered the pressure that racing would apply to snowmobile design!

1963	
★★★★✔	R-6
★★★★	R-8
★★★★★	RD-8

1963

Bombardier's model designations in the early years seemed rather strange, a kind of code that changed from year to year. The models for 1963 introduced the "R" series but the reference to the year in the model designation was dropped and the horsepower of the engine used in each model was added. The "R" designation stood for "Rotax," the Austrian engine builder with whom Armand had made an agreement to supply him engines for use in Ski-Doo. Rotax agreed to supply only Bombardier with engines for use in snowmobiles in North America. Starting with the 1963 models through today, only Rotax engines have been used in Ski-Doo. For 1963, a 163cc, 6hp engine and a 247cc, 8hp engine would be used. The 1963 operator's manual and some literature of the time list the 163cc engine as producing 7hp rather than 6hp. The model designation, R-6, stands for Rotax, 6hp. Perhaps it was assumed the smaller of the new Rotax engines would produce power equal to the 148cc JLO and the model number was assigned on that basis. Was finding an extra horsepower from the 163cc Rotax engine unexpected? Apparently it was. A letter dated November, 24, 1962 from Alphonse-Raymond Bombardier to the distributors noted:

"Gentlemen:

"Experiments made recently on the ROTAX engine which we had announced as a 6hp engine have enabled us to establish that this engine can develop over 7hp.

"We are convinced that your customers will be extremely pleased with the R-6 SKI-DOO which offers the best combination of power, light weight, ease of starting, and low price..."

The arrival of the Rotax engine was only the beginning of what was new for 1963. The Rotax engines would be fitted in a completely new chassis. The "R" models shared a new, super-light chassis and the complete machine weighed in at 135lb when equipped with the 163cc Rotax. The R-6 was equipped with the 163cc Rotax engine while the R-8 utilized the 247cc Rotax, which was equipped with a decompressor valve in the cylinder to reduce cylinder pressure for easier starting.

The engine size, drive pulleys, engine mounting hardware, and exhaust systems were the only differences between the two "R" models. The 163cc engine was fitted with a pulley that had sheaves 5 7/8in in diameter while the 247cc engine mounted a pulley with 7 1/2in diameter sheaves.

The track suspension was the light-weight, small-wheeled system used so successfully the previous year. The track was the endless, 15x114in rubber track with steel reinforcing rods that was making Ski-Doo famous. Cotton was still being used as the reinforcing fiber in the tracks. The chassis tunnel was stamped from a single piece of sheet steel, then formed in a hydraulic press. A steel belly pan was welded into place underneath the front of the tunnel, forming a wonderfully rigid frame and enclosing the 3 imperial gallon (imp gal) container used as the fuel tank.

The new, sleeker-shaped hood or cab for the "R" model Ski-Doos was fabricated in fiberglass and riveted to the steel frame. Just behind the standard windshield was a small tool compartment built into the fiberglass hood. The serial number tag was fastened to the cover on the tool compartment. A fuel tank filler neck penetrated through the fiberglass hood and was fitted with a cap that could be used to measure oil for mixing with the gasoline. Because the new Rotax engines were equipped with a separate generating coil in the magneto, lights were powered by a lighting coil and operated at 12v. A chrome-plated housing held a sealed beam headlight that mounted on the fiberglass hood just above the Bombardier logo. A small taillight assembly mounted on the top of the tunnel, just behind the seat backrest. An on/off switch for the lights mounted on the dash of the hood. Like all Ski-Doos built to that point, the engine was shut down by pushing on the engine shorting button mounted on the engine.

The Rotax engines used on the "R" models had a cast aluminum recoil starter housing. It is one of the ways to verify the authenticity of an original "R" model engine. The problem with the starter was that the rope sheave was somewhat smaller in diameter

The first production twin-track Ski-Doo was a 1963 model dubbed simply the "RD-8". *Lance Parthe*

than later designs and most were replaced with the later recoil assembly which had a steel housing and a larger diameter rope sheave. The later design made starting the engine considerably easier and many owners replaced the originals.

Each "R" model was equipped with a brake. It was a simple pivoting arm design that mounted near the top of the chaincase. A cable connected the arm to a small lever on the front, left side of the handlebar. When pulled, the pivoting arm pressed a brake pad against the fixed half of the driven pulley. The pulley sheave itself was used as the brake disk.

Bombardier unveiled another all-new Ski-Doo in 1963, the "RD-8." The "RD" stood for Rotax-Dual and it was fitted with the 247cc, 8hp Rotax engine. The new model was fitted with two 15x114in tracks and sported a single wide ski. The use of a single ski grew out of Armand's experiences with his twin-tracked prototypes. The single ski didn't turn as easily as his twin ski version but the traction remained much better on the twin tracks with the single, centered ski. It was also found that the single ski was a huge advantage when pushing through brush because it

19

could push through without the brush catching between the skis and the chassis. The "RD-8" was proudly introduced as a machine that offered increased traction, larger track bearing area, longer cruising range thanks to its 6imp gal fuel tank, storage space under the seat for gear and supplies, and increased riding stability.

The "RD-8" weighed 377lb, 147lb more than the "R-8" and utilized the same engine. Top speed of the "RD" was about 22mph but the increased traction and stability instantly attracted a loyal group of customers. The "RD" was defined as a utility version of the Ski-Doo and caught on quickly with cabin owners who wanted to haul supplies to their snow-bound locations and hunters and fishermen bringing gear to remote areas. With a ground pressure of only 0.21lb/sq-in, the RD-8 could break trail through almost any deep snow condition.

The only graphics on the R's and the RD was the name, "Bombardier", in script on the hood with the triangular, "Ski-Doo" beneath. There were no ventilation holes in the hoods of the R models in 1963. Total production for the 1963 "R"s was 5,263.

1964	
★★★	AR-64
★★★	BR-64
★★★	RD-64

1964

Each Ski-Doo got a new model number for 1964. The R-6 became the AR-64 which was actually carried over into production, the R-8 became the BR-64 and the RD-8 became the RD-64. There were few changes between the 1963 and 1964 models. Both the 163cc engine used in the AR and the 247cc engine used in the BR and RD were equipped with plastic air silencers and the 247cc engine was equipped with a centrifugal advance mechanism in the magneto that advanced the ignition timing after the engine was started. The

247 engine received a new, full-circle crankshaft to reduce engine vibration and increase crankcase compression. The combustion chamber shape of the cylinder head was changed to increase low speed torque and the piston was given a different cam grind and more clearance. An isolating flange was installed between the cylinder and the carburetor, eliminating the vinyl connecting tube used on earlier engines. The recoil starter used on the 247 was all-new for 1964. The rope sheave diameter was increased for easier starting and a new sheet metal housing was used. A new muffler, designed by Rotax, was mounted at the exhaust port of the engine and exhausted through a flex pipe that exited just ahead of the footrest. Changes made to the 247cc Rotax engine boosted power to 9hp for the 1964 models.

The upper portion of the fiberglass hood was redesigned for 1964 to "give a smoother line and increased beauty." The hood was fastened to the all steel chassis using 5/32in bolts and speed nuts. The tool compartment/glove compartment in the dash area of the hood was made larger. Another change made for the 1964 model year was the addition of a serial number stamped into the top of the chassis beneath the engine support. Theft of Ski-Doos was increasing with their popularity and the serial number tag on the glove compartment door could be easily removed. This additional identification number helped recover many stolen Ski-Doos.

Suggested retail price for the RD-64, F.O.B. Valcourt, Quebec, in Canadian funds, was $895.00, while the BR-64 retailed for $750.00. The BR-64 and RD-64 were the only new production offerings for the 1963-1964 model year. A letter dated August 20, 1963, and penned by the new Sales Manager for Bombardier, Gaston Bissonnette, noted:

"We have a limited quantity of model R-6 left which we are offering you at the same price as last year and which can be delivered immediately. When the supply of R-6 is exhausted this model will be discontinued."

The R-6 models sold for the 1963-1964 model year were listed as model AR-64 in the operator and parts manuals for the 1964 model year. To further confuse identification of models in the early years of Ski-Doo, Bombardier sold Ski-Doos without engines outside of Canada. Because Bombardier was using either US- or European-made engines, there were import/export advantages and shipping weight advantages in purchasing Ski-Doos without engines. Distributors in Europe and the United States would install the engines at their locations. It is possible to have a completely original 1964 model equipped with a Kohler engine and labeled a BK-64. This machine is somewhat of a mutant, however, for it was never produced that way in Bombardier's plant. Production for the 1964 model year reached 8,532 total units.

Bombardier Snowmobile Limited enjoyed another banner year of sales with the 1964 model Ski-Doos but it was not a year of celebration. The little village of Valcourt lost the creator of the company and inventor of the Ski-Doo. Joseph-Armand Bombardier died of cancer on February 18, 1964, at the age of 56. Armand's eldest son, Germain, took over as president upon his father's death, and Laurent Beaudoin, who was serving as comptroller, was named general manager of the corporation. In 1966, Beaudoin was named president of Bombardier Snowmobile Limited, a position he held until 1979, when he became Chairman and Chief Executive Officer of Bombardier Incorporated, a position he holds to this day.

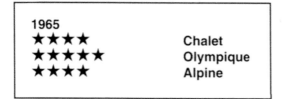

1965

Sales for the Ski-Doo were nearly doubling every year and there was as much effort going into increasing production at the Bom-

bardier plant as was going into development of new Ski-Doo models. Significant for the 1965 model year was the use of model names for the new machines. The AR-64 became the Chalet, the BR-64 became the Olympique and, curiously, the RD-64 became the Alpine. It's interesting that the name first associated with Bombardier's smallest machine became attached to the largest Ski-Doo when it was decided to use model names. Perhaps it was the RD's incredible ability in alpine conditions that encouraged the swap.

The most recognizable change made to the 1965 model Ski-Doos was the new, fiberglass hood with the raised "V" shape just above the fuel filler neck. The "V" was perforated to allow ventilation of the engine while not allowing snow in. The Chalet retained its 163cc Rotax engine while the Olympique and Alpine received the 247cc engine. The only changes to the engines from the previous year was the use of a caged needle bearing rather than a flat bushing on the piston pin and a straight PTO shaft on the 247cc engine.

The Olympique and Alpine received a key-operated light and ignition switch. The Chalet still had the kill switch mounted on the engine and the headlight switch on the dash. Olympique and Chalet models received a three-leaf ski spring replacing the previous two-leaf design. Many improvements were made to strengthen the suspension and steering components and the Alpine got a pivoting arm brake and a fiberglass skid pan to protect the fuel tank, which was still part of the frame.

The Alpine weighed 371lb and had a suggested retail price of $895.00 (FOB Valcourt). The Olympique weighed 250lb and retailed for $750.00, while the Chalet, which shared the same chassis as the Olympique, weighed 230lb and retailed for $650.00. The standard color for all three models was... yellow! Total Ski-Doo production for the 1965 model year was 13,259 units.

The—Gasp!—Blue Ski-Doo!

I've never heard a matter-of-fact definition of how the early Ski-Doos ended up being yellow with a burgundy colored seat cushion. Most stories note that Armand was building large, 12-passenger snowmobiles, often used as school buses, and equipment used by utility companies at the time the Ski-Doo was being developed. The "safety yellow" was commonly used on these vehicles and the seats were often upholstered with the burgundy vinyl material seen on the early Ski-Doos. The yellow color stood out well on the snow and the paint was on hand, so why not use it on the Ski-Doo?

In December of 1964, Laurent Beaudoin had a designer from Quebec City doing some interior design work for him in Valcourt. The designer, Anselme "Sam" LaPointe, had seen the Ski-Doo on his visits to Valcourt and was constantly teasing Beaudoin about how it reminded him of a bulldog. Beaudoin put up with Sam's good-natured teasing for a while, then decided to see if Sam could work some of the same magic he'd seen him do with so many other design projects. Beaudoin, then General Manager of Bombardier Snowmobile Limited, challenged LaPointe to show him what he could do for Bombardier by designing what could become a 1966 model Ski-Doo.

LaPointe accepted the challenge and completely reworked the look of the single-track Ski-Doo. He was ready for his presentation to the board in Valcourt. Sam was confident in what he had to show the executives but waited somewhat nervously as they sat down in front of his veiled prototype. The time had come for Sam to show his creation. I'm sure there were gasps in that room when Sam uncovered a Mediterranean blue Ski-Doo with white stripe and black seat and backrest! The machine was much sleeker looking than previous Ski-Doos. The bulldog look was gone and it even had a retractable headlight so the line of the hood was unbroken but... blue. Beaudoin and the other executives seemed taken with the shape LaPointe had developed but... blue. There were then almost 30,000 Ski-Doos on the planet and they were all yellow. By the time the meeting concluded, it was clear to Sam that Ski-Doo would remain yellow, at least for now. The color was almost a trademark and, like its name, it was part of what made Ski-Doo a Ski-Doo!

Sam had the prototype repainted yellow, changed the white stripe on the hood to black, added the name Ski-Doo in italicized, all-lower case letters in white inside the black stripe, and retained the black vinyl seat and backrest. The new design was accepted and made its debut as the 1966 model Ski-Doo.

The blue Ski-Doo was given one more important showing. A Ski-Doo distributor meeting was held in Salzburg, Austria, in April of 1967. The distributors were given the opportunity to tour the Rotax factory in Gunskirchen and to consider a color change for Ski-Doo as well as see the coming season's new models. As was the case with its unveiling in Valcourt, the blue Ski-Doo generated a lot of discussion. The meeting ended, however, with an agreement among the distributors to retain yellow as the color for Ski-Doo.

LaPointe joined the staff at Bombardier in December of 1968 and has been involved in the aesthetic design of every Ski-Doo and many other Bombardier products since. LaPointe's designs so set the trends in the snowmobile industry that many of the competition's models looked like they were designed by Sam a year after he did them for Bombardier. His son, Denys, joined the staff several years ago and now heads the Industrial Design Department for the entire Ski-Doo/Sea-Doo division.

Model names were used for the first time on the 1965 models. Here the speedy Olympique is shown with an accessory bumper installed. Note the raised, perforated "V" on the hood. *Snow Goer Magazine*

Chapter 2

The Alpine

1965

The very first model name used, at least internally, by Bombardier, Alpine, has remained in the Ski-Doo line up every year since. When first used in reference to the 1962 model, the name referred to the smallest, lightest Ski-Doo in the line. In 1995 the Alpine has grown into the 780lb, twin-track workhorse of the Ski-Doo model line.

To the snowmobiling public, the Alpine has always been known as a twin-track model starting with the 1965 Alpine. This was the year Bombardier started using model names on their Ski-Doo line and assigned "Alpine" to the twin-track model which is used to identify the twin-track to this day.

1966
★ ★ ★ ★   Alpine

1966

The 1966 Alpine received all-new styling to go along with the restyled Olympique model. There was no way the Alpine could have retained the earlier "bulldog" look while the sleek, new Olympique was introduced! Like the Olympique, the Alpine had a retractable headlight assembly. The 1966 Alpine was the last to have the glove/tool compartment in the

1965 Alpine	
Chassis	One piece, all steel
Cowl	Reinforced fiber glass
Dimensions	
Length of chassis	73in
Overall length with ski	96 1/2in
Width of chassis	35in
Height without windshield	36 1/2in
Track & Suspension	
Track	2 endless, rubberized
Width of track	15in each
Length of tracks on ground	50in
Total length of each track	114in
Number of rubber supporting wheels	28
Drive sprockets	4
Suspension	On tandems and springs
Drive	Roller chain in oil bath
Transmission	Automatic, belt and sheaves
Throttle	Hand operated on steering handle
Brake	Hand operated on steering handle
Engine	2-cycle, 1 cylinder, air cooled, 250cc displacement
Weight & Performance	
Weight	377lb (approx.)
Bearing surface	1804 sq-in
Ground pressure	0.21lb/sq-in
Maximum speed	20mph
Seating capacity	2 adults
Approx. gas consumption	1/2imp gal/hr
Miscellaneous	
Fuel tank capacity	6imp gal
Chain case oil capacity	1/2imp pt
Tool compartment	built-in on dash
Storage compartment under seat	33x15x6in

THE POWERFULL ALPINE

The longest-running model name used on any snowmobile began with the 1965 Alpine. To this day, the twin-track Ski-Doo carries the Alpine name.

dash area behind the windshield. There were no louvers in the hood of the 1966 Alpine. The backrest was made easily removable and could be installed in one of two positions on the sled.

The 1965 Alpine had received a fiberglass belly pan to help protect the fuel tank which was in the nose of the chassis ahead of the tracks. For 1966, the fuel tank was removed from the belly pan area of the chassis and a 6 US gallon polyethylene fuel tank was installed on top of the chassis under the nose of the hood. A fiberglass belly pan was then used to enclose the bottom of the chassis where the fuel tank had previously been.

The 1965 Alpine utilized a cast iron cylinder, 247cc Rotax engine, producing about 10hp at 4800rpm. The new, 247cc engine used an aluminum cylinder with cast iron liner with more

"radical" port timing and mounted twin, Tillotson HL carburetors. The new engine produced 14hp at 5800rpm.

Dimensions on the 1966 Alpine remained almost identical to those of 1965. The length of the chassis grew from 73in to 78in but the overall length, including the ski, remained unchanged at 96 1/2in. With the use of the plastic fuel tank, fiberglass belly pan, and aluminum cylinder engine, the total weight remained at about 377lb.

1967	
★★★	Alpine
★★★★⸝	Super Alpine

1967

There were two Alpine models for 1967, both receiving new engines. The standard Alpine received the new, 299cc engine with a single, Tillotson HR carburetor producing 12.5hp at 5200rpm while the Super Alpine was equipped with the first twin-cylinder engine used on Ski-Doo. The twin was a 368cc, opposed-cylinder configuration that mounted a single Tillotson HD carburetor on the rear cylinder. The new twin produced 18hp at 5200rpm and was equipped with an electric starter. The 370, opposed twin-cylinder engine had the crank pins 180° apart, which meant both cylinders came to top dead center at the same time. Even with its large diameter recoil starter sheave the engine was a bear to pull over, which was probably the reason this model became the first electric start Ski-Doo.

Other than the engine, electric start, and engine mounting parts, the only other difference between the Alpine and Super Alpine was the use of a chrome-plated ski holder or bumper and handlebars on the Super Alpine versus a painted version on the Alpine. Non-skid foot pads were added to the top of the tunnel of both Alpine models. Both models received metal louvers in the hood, the headlight was mounted in a fixed position, and the hood was made easily removable with the use of an over-center latch on each side. The ski was reinforced, polyurethane drive sprockets replaced the former rubber type, and the Alpines received the first cam-action driven pulley to replace the former pin type. Also new for the 1967 Alpines was a cable-operated brake caliper working on a separate brake disc mounted on the driven pulley shaft. With

Above and next page: Serial number tags on Rotax engines note whether engines were produced before and after the Bombardier buy-out of Rotax in January of 1970. *Lance Parthe*

the new brake and driven pulley designs came a new chaincase using a double-row roller chain for the first time. Both Alpines gained some weight for 1967, with the Alpine going up to 395lb and the Super Alpine to 425lb.

1968	
★★	Alpine
★★⁀	Super Alpine

1968

There were few changes to the Alpine for 1968. One significant change was to the steering mechanism. Previously, all dual-track models utilized a long ski leg that connected to the ski spring coupler on one end and the handlebars on the other. It took a good pair of arms to steer the machine. For 1968, a method of increasing the driver's mechanical advantage over the ski was employed. The ski leg was shortened and a tubular lever mounted perpendicular to it at the

top of the leg. The steering shaft from the handlebars was fitted with a lever at its end that mounted a ball. The ball fit into the tubular lever at the top of the ski leg. As the handlebar was turned off center, the combination of lever arm lengths amplified the torque applied at the handlebars. Both Alpine models received this clever steering system referred to as the "power link."

The Super Alpine received a new hood sporting dual, 17 watt (w) sealed beam headlights. The lights were recessed into the hood just above the black stripe and clear acetate lenses covered the recesses in the hood to keep snow from accumulating. The Alpine was fitted with the single headlight hood similar to the previous season's. For the first time, nylon was used as the reinforcing cord in the tracks.

1969	
★★	Alpine 370/E
★★	640
★★★	640 ER

For 1973, the Alpine was given "pickup truck" ability with a large cargo area behind the seat. It was the final year for the short-track Valmont. *Bombardier Corp.*

1969

There were four Alpine models offered for the 1969 model year. There was a manual start and electric start version powered by the type 370, opposed twin-cylinder engine, and two versions powered by the all-new 635.1cc type 640 engine. The 640 was a vertical twin-cylinder design with a belt driven, axial cooling fan. Both 640 models of the Alpine were equipped with electric start but the Alpine 640ER also had a reversing gear box designed and built by Rotax. This was the first Ski-Doo model to be equipped with reverse. The new 640 engine produced 40hp and breathed through a single Tillotson HD carburetor.

There was some restyling done for the 1969 model year. Large vertical louvers were set into each side of the hood above the black stripe. The nose of the hood was rounded and broadened and a yellow tinted windshield was used. The weight of the Alpine 640ER went up to 513lb, making it the biggest, heaviest Ski-Doo built to that date.

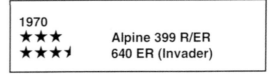

1970	
★★★	Alpine 399 R/ER
★★★♩	640 ER (Invader)

1970

For 1970 the Alpine 640ER's name was changed to "Invader." The Invader was nearly identical to the previous season's Alpine 640ER model. The opposed twin-cylinder 370 became history with the advent of the 1970 models. The new engine for the Alpine was a vertical twin-cylinder, axial fan-cooled 399, producing about 26hp. The engine was equipped with electric start on the "E" model. All three twin track models for 1970 were equipped with the forward/reverse gear box.

| 1971 ★★★ ★★★ | Alpine (all models) Valmont (all models) |

1971

The name game being played with the twin tracks continued for the 1971 model year. The name "Invader" disappeared altogether from the twin track to be replaced by "Valmont." The Valmont moniker was given to the twin tracks that utilized a chassis similar to the 1970 twin tracks, that is, the chassis was equipped with dual, 15x114in tracks. A brand-new dual-track chassis was introduced for 1971. This new chassis mounted two 15ix139in tracks and was given the Alpine name. An additional set of bogie wheels was added on the long track to support the extended length added by the new tracks. There were a total of six Valmont and Alpine models for 1971. All six were equipped with reverse, and a 399 or 640 engine was available in either chassis. The 640 engine was equipped with electric start whether used in the Alpine or Valmont chassis but the 399 was available with or without electric start on either model. Weight on the Alpine 640ER crept up to 578lb, and its overall length stretched out to 113 3/4in. Width on the new chassis remained unchanged at 35in.

One of the developments introduced for the 1971 model year was a new profile for the track lug. Previously, the rubber molded over the track's reinforcing rods was simply round, not offering a lot of traction or "lift" in the snow. The new design had a much longer lug that was angled toward the front of the machine. The long lug offered more traction and the angle helped "plane" the machine up onto soft snow. The new profile track first appeared on the twin tracks and all other Ski-Doo models for the 1971 model year.

The styling was new with a longer, more pointed nose on the hood and a chrome-plated ski holder or bumper. The hood was attached with four over-center latches. A black stripe, highlighted at its edges with a white pin stripe, wrapped all the way around the hood. The Ski-Doo identification was on a separate plastic emblem above the stripe. At the rear of the emblem on both sides of the hood was a safety reflector. This safety reflector/Ski-Doo identification label was used on all models in 1971 and was the first side reflector design used on Ski-Doos. A console enclosed the engine, helping to reduce the sound level at the rider's ear.

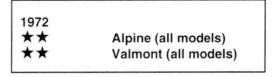

| 1972 ★★ ★★ | Alpine (all models) Valmont (all models) |

1972

For 1972, a 436.6cc, type 434 engine replaced the 399 on both the Valmont and Alpine models. It was offered with or without electric start while all 640s were again electric start. Electric start and manual start models had been equipped with 75w lighting coils until the 1972 model year. For 1972, the 640 received a 120w lighting coil. All six Valmont and Alpine models again had reverse.

The running board area of the tunnel was fitted with six non-slip rubber cushions running the length of the exposed tunnel. The black stripe on the hood was replaced with a reflectorized decal that ran only on the sides of the hood. The Ski-Doo identification was printed on the decal.

| 1973 ★★★ ★★ | Alpine (all models) Valmont (all models) |

The Alpine II, introduced as a 1988 model, brought slide rail suspension and dual 16.5in-wide tracks to the Alpine. *Lance Parthe*

1973

The 640 Valmont was not offered for the 1973 model year; only the type 434 engine, with or without electric start was available on the Valmont. The Alpine was available with the 434 engine or the 640. A pad was added to the handlebars and a 23w lighting coil or "brake light" coil was added to the 75w magnetos to power the new brake light. The Valmont and Alpine also received a high/low beam headlight. Minor changes were made to the graphics on the hood. The seat was shortened on the Alpine and a cargo space enclosed with square tubing was provided behind the operator, making it the first "pickup truck" of snowmobiles. An optional storage compartment with cushion could be added behind the standard seat if two-up seating was required. For the first time, a hydraulic shock absorber was added to the ski.

An interesting exhaust system appeared on the 1973 dual tracks: the snow-cooled muffler. The new sound level limits imposed for 1973 required tighter enclosure of the engine compartment and consequently higher underhood temperatures and a need for quieter mufflers. Ski-Doo engineers came up with a clever design to address both concerns. The basic muffler was enclosed with a second jacket that covered the top and sides of the muffler but was open at the bottom where it was sealed to the chassis with a flexible coupling. Underneath, the jacket was exposed to the high-pressure air flow that exists at the front of the tunnel when the machine is in operation. The double jacket around the muffler lowered the radiated sound and the snow and air mixture flowing between the muffler and the jacket lowered underhood temperatures. A similar design was also used on the 1973 Nordic. Other specifications remained relatively unchanged for 1973. Weight of the Alpine 640ER for 1973 was 610lb.

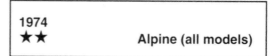

1974
★★   Alpine (all models)

1974

The Valmont with its 114in long tracks was dropped from the Ski-Doo line up for 1974, only the Alpine with its twin 139in long, 15in wide tracks was produced. The Alpine was again offered with 440 and 640 engine sizes, all were equipped with reverse and electric start.

1975

There was virtually no change in the Alpine for 1975 other than the installation of a square shaft, roller clutch on the 640 engine and the elimination of the 440 engine size. The Alpine was given new colors. The chassis was painted black and the hood was given an all-new color, "Orange Ice." The orange ice color continues on the Alpine II to this day.

1976

The 1976 Alpine 640 ER received a new hood design with a column of large louvers on either side of the headlight. A new, square shaft clutch with an idler bearing on the shaft was added for 1976, and little else changed for the year or for that matter until 1980.

1980

The 1980 Alpine was the first to receive a 34mm Mikuni, float-type carburetor. Other than minor reinforcements and calibration changes, little was done with the Alpine until it received a two forward-speed and one-reverse gear box for the 1981 models year. Alpines were being used more and more for grooming and the low gear range allowed for heavy pulling while grooming, yet the high range allowed for speeds up to about 50mph. The 640 engine was replaced with a type 503, 496.7cc, for the 1983 model year. With the new 503 engine came a three-ramp, square shaft drive pulley with idler bearing.

1988

The Alpine then remained virtually unchanged from 1981-1988 when it was replaced in the line by the all-new Alpine II.

The Alpine II's design was aimed at improving operator comfort, increasing maneuverability and stability, increasing pulling power, and making the machine easier to service. The telescoping front strut offered 5.6in of vertical travel while the all-new slide suspension had 4.5in of travel.

1987 Alpine/1988 Alpine II		
	Alpine	Alpine II
Engine	Type 503	Type 503
Drive pulley	Three ramp, roller	TRA
Gear box	2 forward, 1 reverse	2 forward, 1 reverse
Track (two apiece)	15x139in	16 1/2x139in
Overall width	35.5in	43.5in
Overall length	113.5in	120.6in
Overall height	48.5in	58in
Dry weight	643lb	765lb
Bearing surface	2160 sq-in	2193 sq-in
Suspension, ski	Multi-leaf w/shock	Telescoping strut
Suspen., track	Bogie wheel	Slide rail w/ articulating rear
Fuel tank cap	6gal US	9gal US

The rear 12in of the slide rail assemblies was allowed to pivot up to 20 degrees. If something was hit while backing up, the "articulated" rail could raise up, forming an attack angle at the rear of the tracks. The Alpine II was equipped with a weight-equalizing draw bar. The draw bar attached about 2ft forward from the rear of the machine in a location between the tracks. The drawbar could be locked in an up position or allowed to float up to 4 1/2in up and down.

The Alpine II had a much larger windshield than previous models; adjustable handlebars; heat was ducted from the engine to the rider's feet; and a stabilizer bar linking the suspension assemblies improved traction when pulling heavy loads through turns. The Alpine II was a completely new machine!

```
1989
★ ↗              Alpine II

1990
★ ↗              Alpine II
★ ★ ★ ★          Alpine IV
```

1990

Minor improvements and calibration changes were added to the Alpine II as the design was fine tuned through the 1990 model year. For 1990, another Alpine model would be added, the Alpine IV (the IV is for 4-stroke). The machine was essentially identical to the Alpine II except for its type 508 engine. The 508 was an axial fan-cooled, vertical twin, four-stroke cycle engine, displacing 506.8cc. The engine had a dry sump, and engine oil was circulated through a remote reservoir.

The four-stroke engine was designed as part of a study by Bombardier-Rotax in development of lower emission engines for snowmobiles should regulations ever be imposed requiring lowered HC (hydrocarbon)

emissions. The engine proved to be quite noisy and did not offer the low fuel consumption that was expected. The very flat torque curve of the engine proved to be difficult to clutch, and some starting problems were encountered in low temperature situations. Only fifty Alpine IVs were produced and the model was not offered after the 1990 model year. Thirty-five of the original Alpine IVs were converted to Alpine IIs with 503 engines, leaving fifteen original Alpine IVs in the field. The 1990 Alpine IV is the rarest Alpine ever produced and one of the rarest Ski-Doos ever produced.

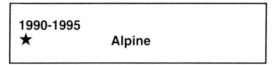

```
1990-1995
★                Alpine
```

1990-1995

Between 1988 and today, the Alpine II has received many calibration changes and modifications to the suspension to change weight transfer characteristics, but the basic design remains relatively unchanged from its introduction. No Alpine model has ever been produced with oil injection. The Alpine and the Élan remain the only pre-mix models in the Ski-Doo line. Because of use in extremely low temperature areas and the problem of keeping oil flowing at temperatures below -40 degrees F, customers in these areas prefer the pre-mix design. It's interesting that the first model name ever used in reference to a Ski-Doo is still in use on a model that grooms trails for millions of snowmobilers around the world.

The 1988 Alpine II's slide rail was articulated at
the rear to ease backing up over obstacles.
Lance Parthe

Identifying Rotax Engines

There has always been some confusion over the identification of Rotax engines. Each engine design is given a "type" number. This number identifies a particular design of engine, and while the type number may approximate the displacement of the engine, it should not be mistaken for the engine's actual displacement, which can be found on the engine serial number tag. Rotax has many engine designs that may have equal or nearly equal displacements. A particular engine is identified by the "type" number. For instance, three engines, all displacing 247cc may be identified as type 247, type 249, and type 250. The 368cc engine used in the 1967 Super Alpine was known as a type 370 engine. Type numbers are also used to identify engines in different states of tune.

Three different serial number tags have been used on Rotax engines through the years they have been used on Ski-Doos. The oldest tag was blue in color and identified the builder as "ROTAX-WERK AG. WELS." The blue serial number tags showed the engine's bore and stroke, displacement, horsepower, and peak horsepower rpm, as well as the serial number of the engine. The variety of engines at this time was not large enough to necessitate the use of a "type" number.

The second serial number tag used by Rotax was black in color and eliminated the horsepower and rpm information, listing only the bore, stroke, and displacement of the engine along with the actual serial number.

The third serial number tag is the one used to this day on Rotax engines. Ski-Doo's incredible growth in sales during the sixties turned Bombardier into Rotax's largest customer. In January of 1970, Bombardier purchased the Lohner company of Vienna, Austria. Lohner held the majority of the shares of Rotax. Bombardier's purchase of Rotax is seen on the latest serial number tag which identifies the builder as "BOMBARDIER-ROTAX GMBH, GUNSKIRCHEN." The new, black serial number tag lists the bore, stroke, displacement, and type number, as well as the engine's serial number. By this point in time, there were so many versions of equal or nearly equal displacement engines that a formal "type" number was needed to identify each.

Chapter 3

The Olympique

1965
★★★★★   Olympique

1965

The model name "Olympique" was first used on the 1965 model that replaced the previous season's BR-64.

1965 Olympique

Chassis	One piece, all steel
Cowl	Fiberglass
Dimensions	
Length of chassis	73in
Overall length	93in
Width of chassis	29in
Height w/o windshield	34 3/4in
Track	Endless, rubberized
Width of track	15in
Length on ground	50in
Supporting wheels	14
Drive sprockets	2
Suspension	Tandems and springs
Drive	Roller chain in oil bath
Transmission	Automatic, belt and sheaves
Throttle	Hand operated on steering handle
Brake	Hand operated on steering handle
Engine	2-cycle, 1 cylinder, air-cooled, 250cc displacement, 10hp
Weight	250lb (approx.)
Bearing surface	1020sq-in
Ground pressure	0.24lb/sq-in
Maximum speed	38mph
Seating capacity	2 adults, 1 child
Approx. gas consump.	1/2imp gal/hr
Miscellaneous:	
Fuel tank capacity	3imp gal
Chain case oil cap.	1/2imp pt
Tool compartment	Built in on dash

1966
★★★
★★★↗   Olympique
              Super Olympique

1966

A completely new chassis and hood was designed by Sam Lapointe for the 1966 model Olympique, and two versions of the Olympique were offered, the Olympique and the Super Olympique. The "bulldog" was gone, replaced by a sleek, new cab with retractable headlight and black stripe that circled the entire hood. The only graphic was the name "Ski-Doo" in italicized, lower case lettering and printed in white within the black stripe. The hood and backrest were covered with black vinyl.

Both the Olympique and the Super Olympique had 247cc engines. The Olympique mounted a 247cc engine equipped with a cast iron cylinder and a single Tillotson HI carburetor. The cast iron 247 was simply referred to as the "regular" 250 engine. The "regular" 250 produced 10.5hp at 4800rpm. The "regular" 250's piston mounted three cast iron rings.

The Super Olympique's engine utilized a cast aluminum cylinder with cast iron liner. The engine mounted two Tillotson HL carburetors on an aluminum manifold, one above the other. The aluminum cylinder 250 was referred to as the AS 250 engine. It was equipped with a two-ring piston and produced 14hp at 5800rpm. The AS and regular 250s shared the

35

The 1965 Olympique weighed in at 250lb and could zip along at 38mph. *J-A Bombardier Museum*

same crankshaft and crankcase; only the top ends and mufflers were different.

Transmissions were identical between the two Olympique models but the Super Olym-pique was geared taller at 10/25 versus the Olympique's 9/26 gears in the chaincase. Both Olympique models for 1966 shared all other features. The approximate weight of the Olympique had gone up only 10lb with the new design for 1966 bringing the total dry weight to about 260lb.

1967	
★★★	Olympique
★★★	Super Olympique
★★★★★	Super 370

1967

Two models of the Olympique were originally introduced for the 1967 model year, the Olympique and the Super Olympique. The Olympique retained the "regular" 250 making 10.5hp, while the Super Olympique received a new, 299cc, type 300 engine. The new engine produced 14.5hp at 5200rpm and was equipped with a single Tillotson HR carburetor. The 250 and 300 shared the same 61mm stroke crankshaft and crankcase but the 300 was given a 76mm bore versus the 250's 69mm bore. Both engines had cast iron cylinders fitted with three ring pistons.

A new twin-cylinder 368cc, type 370 engine was planned for use in the Alpine for 1967. Racing was really taking hold and forcing some considerations in machine design. The longest, toughest cross-country race of the day was the famous Winnipeg, Manitoba, to Saint Paul, Minnesota, event. That particular race and several others had selected a 370cc limit for engines that could be used in the race. With only 165cc, 247cc, and the new 300cc engine available in Ski-Doos, Bombardier was at a disadvantage in the event. The Alpine was not a machine that was going to compete in a cross-country race! Distributors and dealers were aware of the new 370 engine to be used in the Super Alpine and begged that it be installed in an Olympique model. After some discussion with Rotax to see how many engines could be made available, it was decided to produce a quantity of single-track machines powered by the opposed twin-cylinder, 370 engine for the 1967

model year. This was to be the first Ski-Doo produced with competition in mind, and it was competition that forced the first twin-cylinder into the Olympique.

The new model was simply called the "Super 370" and did not carry the Olympique name. Parts books of the time referred to the new model as the "R-16." The engine was identical to the one installed in the Alpine for 1967 but used a different inner fan shroud because it was not equipped with electric start, as was the Alpine. The engine mounted a single Tillotson HD carburetor on the rear cylinder. The carburetor was fitted with an unusual, dome-shaped air silencer. Bore and stroke of the engine was 62x61mm. Cylinders on the

Styling of the 1966 Olympique was a striking departure from the "bulldog" look of the 1965 Olympique. A 10.5hp, cast iron cylinder engine was used in the standard Olympique while the Super Olympique was powered by a 14hp, aluminum cylinder engine with dual HL carburetors.

Bombardier
Ski-doo

SUPER 370

Concerns over competition brought out the opposed twin-cylinder-powered Super 370 for 1967.
Tom Halvorson

370 were cast aluminum with cast iron liners
and the pistons carried two rectangular rings.
One hundred twenty-five Super 370s were
produced by January 7, 1967. It is not known
how many engines were received late in the
model year for installation in additional Super
370s. The Super 370 was equipped with a
nylon cord track, probably the first production model to receive it.

Both Olympique models plus the late-
addition Super 370 model received chrome
plated bumpers and handlebars. The rear
bumper, or grab handle, mounted to the
chassis on a cross shaft, which allowed the
handle to be swung down from its spring
clips and used as a "kick stand" for warm-
ing up the track and keeping the track off

the ground to prevent freezing. Most owners simply leaned the machine on its side
to turn the track over a bit before taking off
and the "kick stand" feature was removed
the following season.

The first kit Bombardier made available
for modifying a Ski-Doo for racing was provided for the 300 engine. The kit was referred to as
"Special Kit For 300cc Rotax For Racing Pur-
poses." The kit included:

"• 1 10-tooth sprocket

"• 1 25-tooth sprocket

"• 1 Heavy duty driven pulley spring

"• 1 Exhaust port flange (To be welded
on the 1 1/2" diameter flexible pipe)

"Instructions:

"Route flex pipe in shortest possible route

The first twin-cylinder engine used in a production Ski-Doo was the 368cc opposed twin producing 17hp at 5200rpm. The engine shown here has been fitted with dual HD carburetors but the original version utilized a single HD mounted on the rear cylinder. *Lance Parthe*

from exhaust port to right side of SKI-DOO just above the black stripe.

"Flexible pipe should be welded on flange (exhaust) then make sure that flex pipe does not come off cowl by securing it with either screw or split pins.

"Recommended spark plug:
"• 280 T1 Bosch if 1 plug
"• 225 T1 Bosch if 2 plugs
"Carburetor:
"• A.S. type (master and slave) 209HL & 210HL by Tillotson."

I have yet to understand what the reference to one or two plugs meant. The note regarding the kit did not use the spark plug's prefix of M (18mm) or W (14mm), which would have helped clear up the confusion. The "master and slave" note regarding the carburetors refers to the progressive linkage arrangement between the twin HL carburetors mounted on the special intake manifold, as was used on the AS 250 engine.

Louvers were added to the nose of the hood within the black stripe. The cable-operated, retractable headlight mechanism was replaced by a lever and rod arrangement. The operating lever mounted in the center on top of the hood behind the windshield, and with its installation, the glove/tool box on the hood disappeared. Stake pockets were added the sides of the track tunnel in 1967 to allow the placement of a backrest behind the driver. Polyurethane drive sprockets replaced the

The 1968 Olympique received a storage compartment in the backrest, which provided a space for the battery on the new electric start model.

The Olympique 299 engine with a sport kit installed was tough to beat on the racetracks. *Halvorson Inc.*

rubber drivers, and nylon lined control cables promised to reduce throttle sticking due to icing. Total production for Ski-Doo rose to 44,421 for the 1967 model year.

1968	
★★	Olympique
★★	Super Olympique
★★★	Super Olympique E
★★★★↙	Super 370
★★★★	Super 370E

1968

The Olympique line grew to five models for 1968, including the Olympique, Super Olympique, Super Olympique-Electric, Super 370, and Super 370E. The Chalet with its 163cc engine disappeared from the line to be replaced by the Olympique as the smallest model in Ski-Doo's line-up for 1968. The Olympique was powered by a reworked 247cc engine producing 11.5hp at 4800rpm while the Super Olympique and its electric start brother were powered by the pumped-up 299cc engine, now producing 16hp at 5400rpm. The 300 engine was equipped with a Tillotson HR carburetor for the first time and was largely responsible for its increase in horsepower over the previous year. The cylinder head of the 300 was new with a more square shape of the fins and the spark plug was inclined toward the rider for easier servicing. The Super 370 and Super 370E were powered by the opposed twin-cylinder, 368cc engine sporting a new ignition system and producing 18.5hp at 5000rpm. Recoil starters on all the engines were painted black for 1968, replacing the silver color previously used.

Perhaps as noteworthy as the engines used in the 1968 Olympique was the installation of the cam action driven pulley. A cam action pulley was used on the Alpine the year before and proved its worth on that hard-pulling vehicle. As power kept increasing with each year, the pin-type driven pulley had to go. The pin-type design simply used three springs pushing against the sliding half of the pulley to maintain pressure on the belt and return the pulley half

Firing Up the 370 Engine

The 370 engine was no fire-breathing racing engine. It made good horsepower for the day but it was an engine with a rather flat torque curve. Peak torque was 13lb-ft at 3700rpm. Starting the 370 was somewhat of a nightmare if you didn't have the "E" version or if your battery was dead, which was most of the time. Because both cylinders came to top dead center at the same time, you had to pull all 368cc through compression at the same time. The 370 was fitted with a recoil with a rope sheave about 1in larger in diameter than the other engines of the time but it was still a bear to pull over, especially when the temperature was below zero. The trick was to close the choke all the way, then open the throttle so that engine vacuum could reach the high speed outlet in the carburetor's venturi. This meant that if you were alone, you had to crank the engine with one hand. Then it was a matter of pulling until the engine fired at least once. At that point you knew you had fuel in the cylinders but it also meant the engine was flooded. Then you would open the choke all the way and hold the throttle wide open until the engine fired and started to clean out. Depending upon the temperature, it was usually a matter of fooling around with the choke in part-open positions to keep the engine running until it gained a little heat. Following this technique, the engine would always start—provided your arm held up! It was always easier starting the 370 when you had another hand available to work the throttle and choke while you had both hands on the starter rope.

Once idling, the 370 shook like mad. Not until you had it turning about 900rpm did it smooth out. Like most clutches of the day, the 370's engaged barely above idle. When the 370 engaged, it started pulling hard right away. It pulled hard right to its peak at 5000rpm and sped you along at close to 60 mph. One of the characteristics of the 370 in the Olympique chassis discovered by the racers who rode it the year before was that the "flat" design of the engine lowered the center of gravity of the machine enough to noticeably improve handling. The 370, as was the case with the other engine designs used in Ski-Doo to that date, were industrial designs adapted to use in Ski-Doo.

when down shifting. The pins that held the springs also transferred torque to the sliding half of the pulley. The design had no way to slow the upshift based on torque requirements at the drive axle and no way to tell the drive pulley to down shift when loads at the axle demanded it to keep the engine from losing rpm. The cam-action design mounted a three-ramp cam with about 38 degrees of angle on each ramp on the sliding half of the pulley. Attached to the driven pulley shaft was what was referred to as the outer cam. It held three plastic sliders that engaged the cam. When drag on the track increased, it, in effect, put the brakes on the outer cam, which pressed on the cam on the

sliding half of the pulley, effectively screwing the pulley shut. This action forced a downshift of the system and the drive pulley had to open up as it reacted to the fixed-length belt. A new, harder compound drive belt with terylene cord was used with the new pulley.

The new, more powerful engines would have simply pulled the drive belt down into the old pin-type pulley, and with their power, the only way they could have downshifted was by getting off the throttle. The new pulley was as much responsible for the 1968's outstanding performance as were the engines.

The tracks for all Olympique models in 1968 were reinforced with nylon rather than cot-

The Olympique 12/3 SS and the Olympique 320 SS were the little brothers of the new T'NT line for 1969. Both SS models controlled their stock classes during the 1968-1969 season. Pictured here is the 1969 Olympique 320. *J-A Bombardier Museum*

A brand new chassis and polycarbonate hood was designed for the 1971 Olympique series. *Halvorson Inc.*

One of the most ambitious snowmobile trips of all time began on March, 28, 1967, aboard six Super Olympic models. Ralph Plaisted of Saint Paul, Minnesota, and five members of his expedition set off from Ellesmere Island in northern Canada for the North Pole. The Plaisted Expedition was forced to abandon their first attempt to conquer the Pole when constantly moving ice and warm weather kept the salt water, which freezes at -40 degrees, from freezing and made passage impossible. The Plaisted Expedition set off again on March 7, 1968, from a point further north, Ward Hunt Island. After a grueling, 43-day trek, Plaisted's expedition arrived at the North Pole at 9:30 a.m., CST, on April 20, 1968. A United States Air Force weather reconnaissance plane witnessed and verified their arrival at 90 degrees North, the point on the planet where every direction you look is south!

1969	
★★	Olympique 12/3
★★	320/E
★★⌐	370
★★★	12/3 SS
★★★	320SS

1969

For the 1969 model year, Bombardier adopted a four-digit code to identify Ski-Doo models. The model code was the first four digits of the serial number and made identification of which model was which much easier than previous systems. Six Olympique models were offered for 1969:

ton fiber. A fiberglass enclosure was added to the backrest, probably to provide a location for the battery on the first electric start Olympique models. While the Olympique had a simple body molding around the base of the hood and the hood was riveted to the chassis, the other Olympique models had a two-piece, stamped, chrome-plated bumper joined at the nose by a rubber bumper. The hoods were fastened to the chassis with four wing nuts on all models above the basic Olympique. The removable hood also had a crash pad in the center area of the dash. Those models were fitted with a chrome-plated, tubular grab handle with passenger grips. The fact that the hood could be removed meant that a tubular frame was needed to support the steering tube, which had previously been mounted to the hood.

All five Olympique models utilized the same basic chassis with differences found only in chaincase gearing, a stronger drive axle on the 370 models (.187in rather than .120in wall thickness), and engine mounting and handlebar mounting differences. Total Ski-Doo production for the 1968 model year was 70,276 and the Olympique was by far the greatest portion of that volume.

Model name	Model number	Engine type	Hp
Olympique 12/3	6910	300	12
Olympique 320	6912	320	18
Olympique 320 E	6913	320	18
Olympique 370	6914	370	19
Olympique 12/3 SS	6916	292	22
Olympique 320 SS	6918	335	26

The chassis for the 1969 Olympique received few changes over the 1968 design. The nose of the chassis was rounded and an all-new, "bullet" nosed, fiberglass hood was designed. Previously, the windshield had been mounted to the hood using a metal strip and screws. The new hood used a rubber strip to secure the windshield into a groove molded in the top of the hood. Tabs at the base of the windshield protruded through the rubber strip and through the hood. Flat metal strips were placed through holes in the plastic tabs of the windshield and folded over the hood to secure the windshield. This design allowed the tabs to straighten out and the windshield to pull off the machine undamaged if it was hit by the rider from behind or an obstacle from the front. The windshield itself was made of Lexan polycarbonate plastic. It was the first safety windshield design Bombardier used. The new hood design also provided more space for the new, larger engines to come. The basic shape and configuration of the all-steel chassis remained relatively unchanged. The lightest of the Olympique models, the 12/3, with its new 299cc engine, weighed in at approximately 285lb.

While all the Olympique models shared essentially the same chassis, the 12/3 was the stripped-down version. There were no front and rear bumpers, the headlight was not retractable, and the earlier, pivoting arm brake rather than the new, self-energizing, drum-type brake was used. All the 1969 Olympique models except the 12/3 received a carburetor equipped with a return line and two fittings were attached to the fuel tank. A portion of the fuel moved by the pump in the carburetor was allowed to flow through the carburetor and return to the fuel tank in an effort to cool the carburetor and reduce the chance of vapor lock.

Snowmobile racing was growing by leaps and bounds in the late sixties. The Olympique SS models for 1969 were produced expressly to qualify for racing in the two smallest stock classes. Stock class limits were set at 295cc and 340cc. The Olympique 12/3 with its 299cc engine was too large to meet the displacement limit and the Olympique 320 with its 318cc engine was a bit short of the 340cc limit. Bombardier worked with Rotax and a cast iron-sleeved aluminum cylinder with a 75mm bore was developed for the 66mm stroke

Lower sound levels were imposed on 1973 models and the new Olympique models met them.

Notice the padded handlebars and fixed headlight positions. *Snow Goer Magazine* engine, and a 78mm bore cylinder was developed for the 70mm stroke, 320 engine. Tillotson HD carburetors were fitted to each engine and port timing was bumped way up. The carbs were fitted with rubber inlet funnels rather than air silencers and the engine's horsepower went way up. The two Olympic SS models absolutely controlled their stock classes during the 1968-69 season and modified versions won more than their share of the mod classes.

Mod kits with the 292 and 335 cylinders along with a carburetor and other necessary parts were available to be fitted to Olympique 12/3 and Olympique 320 models. The kits brought the performance up to the SS version's but were not legal to run in stock class competition. The additional horsepower, however, was welcomed by the kit buyers who snapped them up in large numbers, often racing in the modified classes with their kitted Olympique models.

The Olympique 370 had the lowest production numbers of the Olympique models for 1969 and was a bit of a misfit when compared with all the Olympique models with brand-new engines. While the Olympique was a large percentage of the total Ski-Doo production of 113,227 units for 1969, the Olympique 370 was a tiny number of them, perhaps the lowest production Olympique model ever.

1970	
★	Olympique 12/3
★✦	335/E
★★✦	399

1970

The Olympique selection was reduced to four models for 1970 as the former SS models joined the T'NT line. The Olympique 12/3 returned almost unchanged as the price leader for the entire Ski-Doo line-up. The Olympique 320 was replaced by the Olympique 335, which boasted a 78mm bore like the former SS model but was equipped with a Tillotson HR carburetor. An electric start version of the Olympique 335 was also offered.

Model type	Model Number	Engine type	Hp
Olympique 12/3	7010	300	12
Olympique 335	7012	337	18
Olympique 335 E	7013	337	18
Olympique 399	7014	401	24

The 370 engine became a piece of history as the 399cc, vertical twin-cylinder, axial fan-cooled engine replaced it in the Olympique 399. The Olympique's type 401 engine varied from the T'NT's type 400 engine and produced 6hp less because of its lower port timing, Tillotson HR rather than HD carburetor, and lower compression ratio. Similarly, the Olympique's type 335 engine was a detuned version of the type 340 engine used in the T'NT. It was not the engine used in the previous year's Olympique 335 SS.

The skis were changed in shape for the 1970 model year. A cross section of the ski showed a quite rectangular center section where the wear bar attached compared to the "V" section of the earlier design. The new ski was stronger and provided more aggressive steering. With excep-

For 1977, the 437cc Olympique was called the Olympique 440, not the Olympique Plus as it had been the previous season. *Snow Goer Magazine*

tion of the Olympique 12/3, the Olympique models for 1970 received the previous year's T'NT style hood with a louver on each side above the black stripe. The Olympique 12/3 received the drum type brake that the other Olympique models had received the year before.

The Olympique series was a big seller for 1970 but the expanded T'NT series eclipsed them in total sales. Total Ski-Doo production for 1970 was 181,234 units.

1971	
★★	Olympique 300
★★★↵	300S
★★	335/E
★★★↵	335S
★★	399/E
★★★↵	399S

1971

The 1971 Olympique received an all-new chassis and look. The new chassis would be shared with the narrow track T'NT models. There were a total of ten model numbers assigned to the Olympique series for 1971. Three engine sizes were offered: 299cc, 335cc, and 399cc. The engines were separated from the operator by a plastic console. The single-cylinder 299 was available with bogie suspension or slide rails but all were manual start. The 335 and 399 were offered with any combination of electric start and slide rail or bogie suspension.

The slide rail suspension first offered on the 1971 Olympique models was available the year before on the T'NT models. Marketing referred to the design as the "Ground Leveler Suspension." The system was sometimes referred to as the articulated rail because of its two-piece, jointed rails. The two-piece rails were supported by three suspension arms. The front arm was attached by a cross shaft to the chassis and a bolt pivot at the front of the rail to positively position the rails. The two rear arms attached with cross shafts to the tunnel and to the slide rails on sliding blocks

1971 Olympique	
Overall length	99 3/4in
Overall width	30.6in
Overall height	43in
Weight	327-382lb (option dependent)
Ski stance	24in
Fuel tank capacity	6.25gal US
Track width	15in
Track length	114in

to allow the rails to slide under them as they compressed. There were no shock absorbers in the system. The rear axle attached to the chassis with link plates just like the bogie wheel system. With the rear axle attached to the tunnel rather than the slide rails, there was no reaction of the suspension system to the torque of the engine. This early slide suspension rode better than the bogie wheel system and it was faster but it did not transfer weight to and from the skis based on acceleration and deceleration.

The new chassis was all steel, painted black, and the cab was made of injection-molded polycarbonate plastic rather than fiberglass. The new hood still utilized a retractable headlight to maintain its sleek profile, and the safety mounting of the windshield was retained. The hood was hinged in the front, a first for the Olympique. The new chassis design utilized a polyethylene fuel tank placed in the nose of the machine. The belly pan could now take a pretty stiff thump without rupturing the fuel tank. A two-piece, yellow and black, polycarbonate plastic backrest had storage space that was accessible through a spring loaded door at the rear. The battery for electric start models was removed from the backrest area and located under the hood in the engine compartment. The chaincase was new for 1971. It was still a stamped sheet metal case but the eccentric chain tension adjuster was removed and a spring-loaded, plastic tensioner was added to make chain tensioning automatic. Ski leg bushings were plastic on the new chassis. Passenger grab handles were separate from the rear bumper on models so equipped and bolted to the sides of the tunnel at the rear of the machine. The skis were new with tubular grab handles and enclosed spring ends.

45

There were fifty-five model numbers assigned for the Ski-Doo line in 1971. There were all manner of combinations of electric start, slide rail and bogie wheel suspensions, even steel-cleated or all-rubber track choices on the Blizzard series. Production peaked for Ski-Doo with the 1971 model year at 211,927 units!

1972
★   **Olympique (all models)**

1972

Few changes were made to the Olympique for 1972. The same engines were available with the same choices of slide or bogie suspension and electric or manual start. Black decals were added to the slots in the polycarbonate hood, and blue reflective stripes were added to the sides of the hood. The steering tie rod ends were first equipped during production with ball joints on the 1972 models. The overload spring with rubber cushions at each end was added to the ski springs on the Olympique 335 E, 399, and 399 E.

The lighting coil used on almost all models prior to 1972 was a center-tapped design. The center tap connected to ground on the core of the coil and a yellow and red wire was connected to each end of the winding. Manual start models used a connection to one of the yellow/red wires and the other end of the lighting circuits connected to ground. The other yellow/red wire from the magneto was left unused. The load on the circuit was designed to match the output of the coil and no voltage regulator was used.

On electric start models, a simple diode was connected to each yellow/red wire. The half wave output of one diode was fed to the battery for charging and the other powered the lighting circuits. Later models combined the output of the diodes and fed both of them to the battery to increase charging capacity.

Most of the 1972 models received a new "floating lighting coil"; some very early production, manual start models did not. The new coil had no center tap and the wires connected at each end of the winding were yellow and green in color. The new coil allowed use of a full-wave, bridge rectifier, and doubled the charging capacity on electric start models. Manual start models connected one yellow/green wire to ground on the machine and the other to the circuits for lighting. No voltage regulator was used. The single-cylinder, manual start Olympique models used a 40w coil while the twins and electric start models were equipped with a 75w coil.

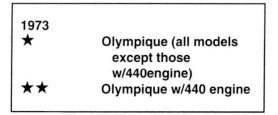

1973
★   **Olympique (all models except those w/440engine)**
★★   **Olympique w/440 engine**

1973

The Olympique for 1973 received a new hood design while the chassis remained relatively unchanged. Gone were the vertical slots in the hood, replaced by a horizontal band that contained the louvers. The headlight was not retractable and protruded above the profile of the hood. The separate, polycarbonate backrest assembly was gone, replaced by a one-piece seat assembly that contained storage space accessed through a door at the rear. The twin-cylinder models had a separate backrest that "plugged" into the rear of the seat on two stand pipes. The 1973 Olympique models also received a cast aluminum chaincase.

There were twelve Olympique models for the 1973 model year, powered by five different engines. The 299cc and 335cc singles, and 399cc twin engine returned from the previous season but the 339cc and 437cc twin-cylinder engines were new to the Olympique line. The Olympique 300 and 335, the single-cylinder models, were not offered with slide rail suspension or electric start. All other models could be purchased with slide or bogie suspension. The 339cc and 399cc engines could be purchased with or without electric start but electric start was not available on the new 437cc twin-cylinder model.

The slide suspension system was a new design for 1973. It featured one-piece rails, a hydraulic shock absorber on the rear arm, and the rear axle attached to the rails. The system still attached the rear of the suspension to the chassis via a pair of link plates but the plates were equipped with sliding blocks that allowed the rail system to slide fore and aft. This design did allow for some reaction through the front arm to the engine's torque but the actual torque reaction was limited.

A new, forged ski leg was used on the twin-cylinder models. This leg attached to the ski with plastic bushings and a special spring coupler that bolted over them onto the leaf springs. A brake light was added to the taillight assembly and a separate, 23w coil was added to the magneto to power it. The main lighting coil on all the Olympique models was 75wo. The use of a separate power source for the brake light kept the lights from dimming when the brake was applied. Manual start models were equipped with a solid state voltage regulator. Electric start models had no voltage regulation. The full output of the rectifier was connected to the battery and the battery itself was used to control output voltage. The Olympique models received a high/low beam headlight along with an emergency shut-off switch. The high/low beam switch and the emergency shut-off switch mounted on the handlebars and protruded through the new safety pad on the bars.

Sound level limits were placed on snowmobiles for the 1973 model year. The Olympique models were fitted with new air

Above (is the 340) and next page (is the 300). For 1975, the all-new Olympique received a chassis that mounted the engine forward, in front of the tunnel rather than on top of it. Two compartments under the hood separated the exhaust system from the engine and used the engine's cooling air to ventilate the forward compartment. *J-A Bombardier Museum*

intake silencers and acoustical foam was attached to the sides of the hood and the engine enclosing console.

1974	
★	**Olympique (all models)**

1974

The Olympique line dropped the 335cc single-cylinder and the 437cc twin-cylinder engines for 1974, leaving a 299cc single-cylinder and the 339cc and 399cc twins. No electric start models of the Olympique were offered for 1974 probably because of carry overs of the previous year's electric

1975	
★★★┙	**Olympique 300/E**
★★	**All other Olympique models**

start models. Olympique models were supplied only with bogie wheel suspension, also probably because of carry overs of slide-equipped models.

1975

The Olympique models were entirely new for 1975, sporting a new, all-steel chassis and new hood design. The new chassis was the first in the Olympique's history to forward-mount the engine and place the fuel tank on top of the tunnel in front of the operator. The single-cylinder, 299cc engine was replaced with a new, twin-cylinder, 295cc engine. The new engine should not to be confused with the physically smaller, 293cc engine then used in the Élan SS. The Olympique's little twin utilized the 61mm stroke bottom end of the type 343 engine and was fitted with 55.5mm bore cylinders. The new engine was offered with or with out electric start as was the only other engine available in the Olympique for 1975, the 339cc, type 343 engine.

1975 Olympique	
Overall length	100.8in
Overall width	33in
Overall height	43in
Weight	339-384lb (option dependent)
Ski stance	26.3in
Fuel tank capacity	6.5gal US
Track width	15in
Track length	114in on Oly 300; 120in on Oly 340

One of the features of the new Olympique chassis and hood design was originally presented in dealer meeting films as "Binary Compelled Cooling" (BCC). The rather clumsy name was later changed to "Tornado" cooling. The system used two compartments under the hood separated by a heat shield or bulkhead that sealed against the inside of the hood. The engine was in the rear compartment and the muffler was in the separate area up front. Cooling air from the engine was ducted into the forward compartment and allowed to escape through the louvers in the hood and openings in the belly pan, one of which was concentric with the exhaust outlet pipe. The idea was to keep the heat liberated from the exhaust system away from the engine and use the engine's cooling air to cool the exhaust system compartment. Controlling engine heat became more and more of a concern as the engines became more tightly enclosed in an effort to lower sound levels of the machines.

The Olympique 300s were both equipped with bogie wheel suspension while the 340s received a new torque reaction suspension similar to what had been on the T'NT fan-cooled models the previous year. The new suspension produced, by far, the best riding Olympique to date and was the reason the new 120in track was used on the 340s only. The bogie suspended 300s used the 114in track from the previous year. The 1975 Olympique models were the first ones to receive hydraulic shock absorbers on the skis.

A new self-adjusting disk brake replaced the drum brake previously used on the Olympique models. A two-roller, square shaft clutch replaced the earlier, four-fly-

weight design. A primer was added to make cold starting easier and the fuel pump was separated from the carburetor to reduce the chance of vapor lock on both the 300 and the 340. The 75w/23w lighting coil/brake light coil combination was replaced by a single 100w coil. The 1975 Olympique models were indeed new from the wrap-around aluminum bumper up front to the padded steel bumper at the rear.

1976	
✈	**Olympique 300 M**
★✈	**Other Olympique models**

1976

The Olympique line expanded to six models for 1976. A single-cylinder 299cc engine returned in what was labeled the Olympique 300 M. The "M" stood for Mono. Also returning was a 437cc engine in what was called the Olympique Plus. The Mono and the Plus were available in manual start versions only. The Olympique 300 and 340 returned in manual and electric start versions. The 300 was referred to as the 300T to avoid confusion with the single-cylinder version.

The Olympique 300 Mono was an economy model and was stripped of some of the features of the other Olympique models for 1976. It used the old, four-flyweight, round shaft clutch, and the earlier drum brake design operating on a flange stamped on the fixed half of the driven pulley. The skis did not have shock absorbers, and, because the single still used a 75w lighting coil, the machine did not have a voltage regulator. The 300 M and 300 T were both equipped with bogie wheel suspension and a 114in long track while all other models rode on slide rails and a 120in long track.

1977	
★	**Olympique (all models)**

1977

The electric start version of the Olympique 300 T was dropped from the line leaving five Olympique models for 1977. The 300 M kept its Tillotson HR carburetor from the previous season but all twins were equipped with Mikuni VM, float-type carburetors. The 300 T and 340s were equipped with 30mm Mikunis while the 440 got a 32mm version.

The 437cc Olympique was called the Olympique 440 for 1977, not the Olympique Plus, as it had been the previous season, and it had a new engine. The previous engine was a type 434 while the engine for 1977 was a type 440 engine. The engines had the same bore and stroke, therefore the same displacement but there were many differences between the two engines. One difference, the larger diameter fan and fan housing, made things a bit too cramped under the hood. Rather than tool for an all-new hood, a raised louver was designed that fit over an opening cut in the polycarbonate hood. The louver was held on by four push nuts and allowed air directly into the fan housing.

The 300 M was set up with a round shaft, two-roller clutch. Both 300s stayed on bogie wheels while the 340 and 440 rode the rails. Other changes to the 1977 Olympique models were minor.

1978 ★	Olympique (all models)

1978

Declining Olympique sales cut the number of models back to three for 1978. One bogie-equipped model powered by the 300 twin, manual start engine was offered, and electric and manual start versions of the slide-suspended 340 were made. Other than minor graphics updating, the Olympique models were mechanically unchanged for 1978.

1979 ★★★✈	Olympique both models

1979, The Final Olympique

The 300 twin was dropped and the final year of the Olympique offered a manual or electric start version of the 340 only. Both were equipped with torque reaction slide suspension and the 120in long track. The Olympique chassis and skis were painted gray for 1979 to match the rest of the Ski-Doo line. No technical changes were made for the final year. The first two years of the Citation, 1978 and 1979, were built on a shortened version of the final Olympique chassis but that first Citation model would also disappear with the 1979 model year.

Chapter 4

The Chalet

1964-1967
★ ★ ★ ★   **Chalet**

1964

Chalet was the name given to the model dubbed the R-6 of the preceding year. It was the smallest, lightest, most economical Ski-Doo. The Chalet used the same chassis as the Olympique model of the year. The major difference between the two was the Chalet's 163cc Rotax engine versus the Olympique's 247cc engine. Remember that from the model year 1963, "R-6" was to stand for Rotax, 6hp. During testing, however, it was found that the 163cc engine actually produced 7hp. The Chalet's engine was fitted with a smaller, lighter drive pulley that measured 5 7/8in in diameter at the sheave. The Chalet had no ignition switch, only a stop switch mounted on the engine. An on/off switch for the lights mounted on the hood. The Chalet weighed 230lb while the Olympique weighed in at 250lb. Retail price for the Chalet, FOB Valcourt, was $650.00

1965

The Chalet returned for the 1965 model year with the same changes that the Olympique received for 1965. Top speed for the Chalet was said to be 30mph. The year 1965 was to have been the last for the Chalet. This was a concern for some of the Ski-Doo distributors who were worried that without the lighter, less expensive model in the line, sales would be lost to the growing competition. The market was growing by leaps and bounds, and it was the bigger, faster, more powerful models that were in the greatest demand. That was obvious to Bombardier from the carryover of Chalet models at the end of the 1965 model year. One Ski-Doo distributor in the United States purchased a large number of the 1965 Chalets and renamed them "Chateau." They were sold during the 1965-66 model year for $100.00 less than the all-new Olympique model for that year. Chateau was never a model name used by Bombardier.

1967

The Chalet disappeared for 1966 but returned on the all new Olympique chassis for the 1967 model year. The machine retained its 7hp, 163cc engine and its dry weight went up to 240lb. The year 1967 was the last for the Chalet.

Rotax Designs Engines
Expressly for Ski-Doo

The relationship between Bombardier and Rotax had been a symbiotic one in the mid-sixties. Rotax was producing wonderfully dependable, great-performing engines, and they were helping establish Ski-Doo as the unquestioned leader in the snowmobile industry. Bombardier was quickly becoming Rotax's largest customer. Rotax, however, had been supplying industrial design engines or slightly reworked versions of their industrial engines for use in Ski-Doo. The opposed twin-cylinder 370 had been used in industrial applications and had been tested in a small automobile in Europe. It was the first twin-cylinder Rotax used in Ski-Doo but was far from the ultimate in engine design for a snowmobile.

A handful of people, mostly racers, had seen a vertical twin-cylinder 494cc Rotax installed in Ski-Doo as early as 1966. The 494 was another industrial engine produced by Rotax. In its stock configuration it produced 17hp at 4000rpm. The engine was cooled by a large flywheel-mounted fan. A tiny Bing carburetor fed the engine. The cylinders were cast iron and had very low port timing. Bombardier never produced a Ski-Doo model using the 494 engine.

Wajax, a company in Montreal, Quebec, imported Rotax engines for industrial applications. Roger Langlois, a very successful Ski-Doo racer from Montmagny, Quebec, contacted Wajax in 1966, explaining that he was in need of an engine capable of powering a peat moss harvesting machine he was working on. Langlois was able to acquire five 494 engines from Wajax. He knew they weren't going to compete in the unlimited class in their stock configuration.Langlois brought the engines to a friend who was involved, avocationally, in two-cycle engine modification, Jean-Paul Samson.

Samson modified the cylinders, in-stalled dual carburetors and a straight pipe exhaust system, reduced the engine's rotating weight and, on one engine, removed the cooling fan and shrouds to utilize "free air" cooling. Langlois first showed up with the 494 powered Ski-Doo at a race in Quebec City and devastated the competition. The convincing demonstration of the 494 modified by Samson caught Bombardier's attention and they quickly made contact with him. Jean-Paul went to work for Bombardier as their first high-performance engine coordinator in July of 1967. Jean-Paul Samson continues to work today with Bombardier's research and development department.

Word of the 494's outstanding performance at Quebec City spread quickly and 494cc engines started dribbling over the boarder into the United States. A group of motorcycle racers that worked with Sport Cycle Sales in Idaho Falls, Idaho, had been tuning and racing motorcycles with great success when the snowmobile phenomenon exploded onto the scene. Gary Scott was one of the tuners and drivers from Sport Cycle Sales that dove into high-performance tuning of Ski-Doo snowmobiles. Gary was racing a CZ motorcycle at the time and had access to expansion chamber design information and experience through a Czechoslovakian racing technician. The hot set-up for exhaust systems on racing snowmobiles of the time was either a straight pipe about 15in long or a megaphone. To my knowledge, Gary is the first technician anywhere to develop a tuned expansion chamber for snowmobile use. His first pipe was developed for the AS 250 engine and produced dramatic results.

The 494cc engine had the same bore and stroke as the AS 250 at 69mm x 66mm and Gary wanted to use his ported AS 250 cylinders on the 494, but the 250's cylinders had much wider transfer port passages than the stock 494 cylinders. The Sport Cycle

Sales boys sawed the cylinder fins and transfer passages as necessary to fit them on the 494 bottom end then welded plates over the openings they had created in the transfer passages. A set of Scott's pipes were fitted that hung out the right side of the hood. The combination was an incredible success!

Rotax had a high-performance development program underway headed by Helmut Roteh (No connection with the company name. The name Rotax was taken from the Latin word meaning rotating axle.) One of the first competition-oriented products to be made available by Rotax was the 300 Sport Kit. The kit contained a complete top end for the 299cc engine. The piston in the kit had a unique cam grind to reduce the chance of seizure, and it was equipped with a Dykes pattern piston ring. The cylinder head had a smaller combustion chamber for a higher compression ratio. The cylinder was cast aluminum with a cast iron liner and the intake port accepted a Tillotson HD carburetor. The port timing was higher than the standard cylinder and a clever arrangement was provided to allow the engine modifier to gain easy access to the transfer ports. A plate held on by two screws covered the transfer passage on the outside of the cylinder. The plates could be removed and any grinding the modifier cared to try could be easily accomplished. The kit also contained specifications for an exhaust megaphone and an intake funnel to be fabricated by the owner. The kit pumped the 300's horsepower from the stock 16hp at 5400rpm to almost 20hp at 6100rpm

Roteh had a completely new engine design under development expressly for use in Ski-Doo. It was a vertical twin-cylinder engine with a 76mm bore and a 66mm stroke, the same as the 300 engine. The new engine displaced 599cc and was known as the Rotax 600. To make the engine compact and light, the transfer passages were overlapped at the center of the engine by twisting the cylinders on the crankcase, which spaced the exhaust ports further apart at the front of the engine and the intake ports closer together at the back of the engine. The large flywheel-mounted fan of the 494 was removed and replaced by a 7 1/2in diameter fan mounted at cylinder height in a housing on the right side of the engine and driven by a "V" belt from the magneto flywheel. A cooling shroud covered the front and left sides of the cylinders and ducted air from the fan over them and toward the rider. The design became known as an axial fan-cooled engine. The engines were equipped with one Tillotson HR carburetor mounted on a common manifold above one Tillotson HD carburetor. The manifold created a plenum between the intake ports of the cylinder. Since the crankshaft was a 180 degrees design, only one cylinder breathed from the plenum at a time. The carburetors were connected with a progressive linkage to a single throttle cable. The muffler was the standard "can" of the time and definitely was not a tuned system. Waiting in the wings, however, was a new tuned expansion chamber that Gary Scott had developed for the 300!

The stock 600 produced about 40hp at 6000rpm. Modified versions, such as the one Steve Ave used to win the 1968 Eagle River World's Championship using the Sport Cycle Sales pipes, were making about 50hp at 6800rpm. The Rotax 600 was compact and powerful and dominated racing in the unlimited class through 1968. The success on the racetrack was only the beginning of what the 600 would mean to Ski-Doo. The axial fan-cooled design became the design for twin-cylinder and several single-cylinder engines for the entire industry. More important for Ski-Doo, however, was the high-performance model line that the 600 created, the T'NT!

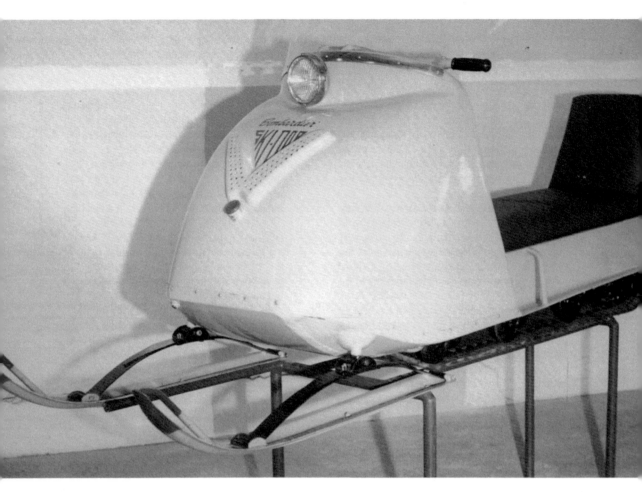

The Chalet was the lightest full sized Ski-Doo ever built and utilized the smallest engine at 163cc. Weighing only 230lbs, it was incredible in deep snow. It was built for the 1964, 1965 and 1967 model years. *J-A Bombardier Museum*

Chapter 5

The T'NT

1968 ★★★★★	T'NT 600

1968

A bulletin dated December 11, 1967, regarding the Rotax 600cc engine was sent to Ski-Doo distributors. The bulletin read:

"A. In the near future a limited number of Rotax 600cc engines will become available.

"B. In order to provide a good engine life you should set up the gear ratio of the Ski-Doo equipped with a 600cc engine in such a way that the engine will not turn higher than 6000 rpm. This is very important.

"C. UNDER NO CIRCUMSTANCES THE ENGINE SHOULD BE ALLOWED TO REV. UP MORE THAN 7000 rpm.

"D. Even if 6000 rpm seems conservative, you have to consider the actual torque curve of this specific engine. Therefore, there is no need to set up the speed of this engine higher than 6000 rpm."

This bulletin from the Service Department seems to suggest that the new 600cc engine was going to be supplied to distributors *sans* snowmobile for installation in a chassis of their choice. Testing of the new engine must have demonstrated that the 600 was just too powerful for any Ski-Doo chassis without some critical beefing up. The bulletin was fol-

lowed by a letter from John Hethrington, Marketing Manager, about two weeks later in regards to: "Conditions of sale for 1968 600cc race Ski-Doos." Hethrington's letter noted that, "600cc Ski-Doos will be shipped complete with engines and billed to distributors..."

The letter quoted wholesale and retail prices for the 600 but never referred to the model as a T'NT. Bombardier was concerned about keeping the new machine out of the hands of the competition and the letter dictated the conditions of sale for each 600. One con-

Rotax produced a handful of reverse rotation engines for competition. This 299cc engine is also fitted with the 300 sport kit. Notice the removable plates covering the transfer ports. *Lance Parthe*

The 599cc vertical twin was the first engine Rotax designed expressly for Ski-Doo, and it was used to power the first T'NT model in 1968. This engine set the standards for virtually all fan-cooled snowmobile engines to follow it. *Lance Parthe*

dition of sale read: "The dealer may only sell the 600cc to a retail customer for the duration of a race and the machine must be resold and returned to the dealer at the end of the race. This condition is to keep the 600cc Rotax engines away from competitive manufacturers."

The earliest printed document I've seen that refers to the new machine by name was a parts supplement dated January 1968. This parts list refers to the machine as the "Track N'Trail-600."

When it was decided to supply the new engine complete with chassis, several strengthening modifications were performed to the Super 370 chassis. An angle iron was placed across the chassis to strengthen the engine mounting area. The ski springs had a leaf added and the ski legs were made stronger. A spreader bar was placed in the rear of the tunnel to strengthen it. The drive axle, which had been hollow on all previous Ski-Doos to allow lubrication of the right side axle bearing by the chaincase oil, was replaced with a solid axle mounting urethane drive sprockets. To center the engine on the chassis, a new beefed-up chaincase, offset to the left, was designed. The new chaincase mounted a pivoting arm brake, used the standard 1/2in pitch, single row roller chain but was fitted with a strengthened driven pulley.

The new hood designed for the 600 was a sign of things to come from Ski-Doo. The hood had two openings at the sides just above the black stripe on the hood. A separate, fiberglass scoop was riveted to the opening, giving the hood a distinctive look. The hood was yellow with a black stripe, typical of all the 1968 Ski-Doos, but centered on the retractable headlight was a large solid black dot. On the hood scoops was a rectangular, red, white and blue decal. In the red area of the decal, "t'nt" was printed in white lower case letters separated with a white vertical stripe from the blue area which contained "600," also printed in white. The entire decal was outlined in white. The windshield was very low and the seat was brand new. There was no backrest on the new seat, only an upholstered "hump" at the rear. A tool storage area was provided at the front of the seat.

T'NT stood for Track 'N Trail, which is why the apostrophe is in the acronym. It was a perfect name for the new model line. It described what Bombardier wanted the model to do, compete on the racetrack and be a fully equipped, hot performer on the trail, while suggesting the explosive power of trinitrotoluene. The introduction of the T'NT with the 600 could have not been more successful, as it dominated the unlimited class across North America. You had to be a recognized racer to climb aboard one, however, for only 117 of them were made!

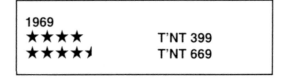

1969	
★★★★	T'NT 399
★★★★✦	T'NT 669

1969

Timing for the T'NT series' formal introduction couldn't have been better set up. Snowmobile racing was growing faster than anyone could have imagined and the T'NT 600's impressive showing in 1968, including winning the Eagle River World's Championship, had the new T'NT line sold out before the 1968-1969 snowmobile season arrived!

T'NT 399/T'NT 669		
	T'NT 399	T'NT 669
Overall length	94in	93in
Overall width	31in	33.75in
Approx. weight	314lb	385lb
Ski stance	24in	27in
Fuel capacity	3.75 US gal	6.25 US gal
Track width	15in	18in
Track length	114in	114in
Bore	64.5mm	78mm
Stroke	61mm	70mm
Displacement	398.4cc	668.6cc
Carburetor	1-HD	1 (stock) or 2-HD
Horsepower	30hp	45hp
Suggested retail price	$1,045	$1,395

Two T'NT models were offered for the 1969 model year and both had brand-new engines. They were dubbed the T'NT 399, which was on a slightly modified Olympique chassis, and the T'NT 669, which shared a new chassis with another new Ski-Doo arrival, Nordic. Both engines were axial fan-cooled, vertical twin-cylinder engines. The 399 mounted a single Tillotson HD carburetor. The 669s were delivered with a single Tillot-

son HD carb, but an intake manifold mounting two HDs, one above the other, was available. The 399 produced 30hp while the 669 made 45hp.

One of the problems race drivers encountered with the T'NT 600 was, with the engine virtually in your lap and no fan shroud on the backside of the cylinders to deflect the heated air away from the rider, the machine was uncomfortably warm to drive. The new engines had two-piece shrouds that ducted the heated air to the left side of the engine and away from the rider.

The T'NT models had no intake silencers, only a black rubber intake funnel based on the dimensions of the intake funnel described in the 300 Sport Kit instructions. Because the engine was on top of the tunnel, right in front of the rider, the intake funnel could be easily hit with a knee while flailing around on the machine in the heat of competition. This is why rubber was selected as the material for the funnel. More than one rider did bump the rubber funnel with a knee, however, turning

The original T'NT was the 1968 T'NT 600, which dominated its class in competition, including picking up the 1968 Eagle River World's Championship with Steve Ave aboard. Only 125 T'NT 600s were produced. *Bill Fullerton*

it into a full choke! After such an experience, many riders removed the inlet funnel rather than risk choking themselves out of a win.

The T'NT 399, using the basic Olympique chassis, received a new chaincase with double-row roller chain and a drive axle with a center idler to reduce rolling resistance. The rear axle also had a center idler. The machine was equipped with a single-shoe drum brake. Bogie wheel suspension was used on both the new T'NT models. The seat on the T'NT models was similar to the 600's with no backrest, only the hump. Tool storage was provided at the front of the seat.

The T'NT 399's hood, secured to the chassis with four wing nuts, incorporated the air intake openings above the black stripe similar to the T'NT 600's but the hood was molded in a single piece. It also inherited the large, black dot centered on the retractable headlight. The yellow-tinted Lexan windshield was mounted with the same safety break-away system as was used on the Olympique models for 1969.

The T'NT 669 was completely new and shared the 18in chassis of the Nordic, which was also introduced for the 1969 model year. The new chassis incorporated a steel belly pan that wrapped up the sides of the machine almost to the height of the seat. The sleek fiberglass hood was hinged in the front, meeting

neatly with the belly pan, the joint covered by a chrome-plated, wrap-around bumper. The T'NT 669 also had center idlers on the drive and rear axles, the humped seat with no backrest and a small break-away windshield. There was no black stripe on the T'NT 669, only a black section in the middle of the hood flowing back behind the windshield. On the sides of the hood above the Ski-Doo name plate was a circular red, white, and blue "t'nt/669" label.

Neither the 399 nor the 669 had tuned exhaust systems, only the "can" muffler exhausting out the center of the chassis in front of the track. Both T'NT models used bogie wheel suspensions but were equipped with stiffer springs than were the Nordic or Olympique models. The T'NT 399, along with the two Olympique SS models, dominated their stock and modified classes during the 1968-1969 season but the T'NT 669 had a tough season against the 800cc competition. For the displacement it gave up in the big mod class, however, the 669 did remarkably well. On the trails, it was *the* machine to have.

1970	
★★★	T'NT 292, 340
★★✦	T'NT 399
★★★✦	T'NT 640, 775

1970

The T'NT line expanded to nine models for 1970. The Olympique SS models were added to the T'NT line as the T'NT 292 and T'NT 340. The T'NT 399 returned but was put on the 18in chassis. The T'NT 640 was a new addition while the T'NT 669 was replaced by the T'NT 775. The T'NT 775 was offered only with slide rail suspension but each of the other T'NT models was available with slide or bogie suspension.

The T'NT 292 and 340 were often listed with the Olympique models on internal memos. The parts books even listed them as the Olympique T'NT 292 and Olympique

The T'NT 600 had the black dot on the hood that became the distinctive mark used on the 1969, 15in T'NT. *Bill Fullerton*

Engine Data for the 1970 T'NT models					
	292	340	399	640	775
Bore	75mm	78mm	2x64.5	2x76	2x82
Stroke	66mm	70mm	61mm	70mm	73mm
Displacement	291.4cc	334.3cc	398.4cc	634.7cc	770.6cc
Carburetor	1 HD	1 HD	1 HD	1 HD	2 HD
Horsepower	22hp	26hp	30hp	40hp	65hp

Above and next page: In 1969, the T'NT 399 and 669 were produced using new engines. The T'NT 399 shared a beefed-up chassis with the Olympique series while the T'NT 669 shared a chassis with the new Nordic model with its 18in-wide track. *J-A Bombardier Museum*

T'NT 340. A memo from John Hethrington dated April 30, 1969, explained the situation to the distributors.

"... From time to time you may receive from Valcourt price schedules or information grouping these series differently. This results from following either production or other considerations in their grouping. For instance on some reports you may find the T'NT 292 and 340 grouped with the Olympique series. This occurs because the production people produce these models on the 15in track assembly line and consider them as one group. As far as yourselves and the Marketing Department are concerned, there will be a considerable difference between the type of market, personality and engine for the T'NT and Olympique series and therefore they should be separated..."

The 15in and 18in chassis were essentially unchanged from the previous year with exception of the addition of Ski-Doo's first production slide rail suspension system on the T'NT models equipped with the $20 slide rail option. The system had been tested by race drivers in the modified classes the previous season and proved to be both faster and smoother riding than the bogie wheel system. The new jointed rail system was called the "Ground Leveler Suspension." The system utilized a jointed rail with no shock absorber and the rear axle and link plate were the same as that used on the bogie wheel systems. The slide rail tracks were the same as the bogie wheel tracks with the exception of the wide insert clip to allow a sliding surface for the high density polyethylene slider shoes.

Restyling of the T'NT models was modest. A black decal was added to the sides of

the hood behind the louvers on the 18in chassis and a circular patch with T'NT on it was added to the sides of the "hump" on the seat.

The 292, 340, and 399 engines received few changes for 1970. The 640 was, basically, the 669 fitted with 76mm bore cylinders and pistons. The 771 was an all-new engine based on the layout of the 669. It used a fan shroud similar to the 1968 600, dumping the engine's cooling air right in the rider's lap. The intake manifold was new, directing the twin, side-by-side Tillotson HD carburetors directly into each cylinder. The common plenum between the cylinders was gone. The 1970 T'NT series would see competition at many events during the 1969-1970 season but much of the glory was to be stolen by the new Blizzard race sleds for 1970.

1971	
★★	T'NT 15in models
★★⌡	T'NT 18in models

1971

The 292 and 340 T'NT models received an all-new chassis for 1971. The all-steel frame was fashioned after the 18in chassis used on the larger T'NT models and the Nordic. The belly ban wrapped on the sides, joining the hood at a chrome plated, wrap around bumper. The built-in fuel tank was gone, replaced with a 6.25 US gallon plastic tank. Support for the ski leg spindle housings was provided by a stamped steel cross member which rose up over the plastic fuel tank, ala the Nordic/18in T'NT design. The seat was tapered from the front to the rear with only a very small hump at the rear. The yellow hood had a raised section in the center that was painted black and joined the windshield in a smooth, streamlined fashion. This raised section also held the tachometer and speedometer where it met the windshield. The hood was mounted with hinges at the front and over-center spring latches held it down at the rear. Retractable headlights disappeared from the T'NT models.

All sizes of the T'NT for 1971 were available with either bogie wheel or ground leveler suspension systems. All T'NT models benefited from the new, deep-profile track, which had an angle on the contact side of the lug that helped "plane" the machine onto the snow. The steel reinforcing rods in the track were 1/4in in diameter. The chaincases were equipped with a spring-loaded plastic slider that automatically tensioned the chain. Skis were all-new with a tubular grab handle rather than the stamped, flat sheet metal handle, and both spring ends were enclosed on the new ski design. The 1971 T'NT models were not originally equipped with ball joints at the tie rod ends. Design changes in the new chassis put a strain on the rod ends and a refit was ordered by Bombardier. The outer tie rod ends were fitted with ball joints like those used on the 1971 Blizzard models.

There was little change to the engines for 1971 but they were all painted black and the 30hp 399 was replaced with a 35hp 437cc engine. The axial fan-cooled, twin-cylinder engine mounted a single Tillotson HD carburetor. The new engine had a 67.5mm bore with a 61mm stroke. In 1970, the Blizzard 292s and 340s could run in the stock classes when fitted with a muffler. None of the 1971 Blizzard models qualified for stock class competition but a high-altitude version of the T'NT models was legal. These engines had a higher compression head and produced better power when run with 100 octane avgas at low altitudes.

1971 T'NT					
	292	**340**	**440**	**640**	**775**
Overall length	99in	99in	100in	100in	100in
Overall width	30 5/8in	30 5/8in	34in	34in	34in
Approx. weight	310lb	315lb	360lb	390lb	430lb
Ski stance	24in	24in	27in	27in	27in
Fuel cap. (US gal)	6.25	6.25	6.25	6.25	6.25
Track width	15in	15in	18in	18in	18in
Track length	114in	114in	114in	114in	114in
Bore	75mm	78mm	67.5mm	76mm	82mm
Stroke	66mm	70mm	61mm	70mm	73mm
Displacement	292cc	335cc	437cc	635cc	771cc
Carburetor	1-HD	1-HD	1-HD	1-HD	2-HD
Horsepower	22	26	35	40	65

Cast aluminum drive pulleys first appeared on the 1971 models, replacing the stamped and welded steel versions. The new pulley had a hole drilled perpendicular to the shaft that allowed grease to weep onto the sliding half bushing when the hollow clutch shaft was packed. It also allowed a cap screw with a grease fitting to be used so the clutch shaft could be greased with a grease gun, greatly cutting down on maintenance time. The pulley halves had alignment marks on them so that the grease hole would not line up with the flyweight notches in the sliding half hub when in high gear position.

1972	
★★★★	**T'NT 400**
★★★⌿	**T'NT 340, 440 specials**
★★⌿	**All other models**

1972

The first Ski-Doo to use a color other than yellow and black as a featured color was the 1972 T'NT. Down the center of the hood was a wide, white stripe set in the black center of the hood. The side panels of the hood were yellow and featured a red, reflectorized stripe with the Ski-Doo identification in it. The fiberglass hood was new for 1972 with a wider center section and windshield. The profile of the hood was lowered about 2in on all but the 292, which, because its tall single-cylinder engine, did not allow it. The chassis remained black.

The single-cylinder 335cc engine was replaced with a twin-cylinder, axial fan-cooled 339cc engine mounting a single Tillotson HD carburetor. Making its debut on the new little twin was the first tuned muffler to be used on a T'NT model. Only the 1970 292 and 340 Blizzard models had used a tuned muffler before the 1972 T'NT models. All other mufflers used had only been concerned with lowering

1972 T'NT models						
	292	**340**	**400**	**440**	**640**	**775**
Overall length	99in	99in	99in	99in	101in	101in
Overall width	30 5/8in	30 5/8in	30 5/8in	30 5/8in	34 1/2in	34 1/2in
Approx. weight	316lb	328lb	410lb	356lb	400lb	440lb
Ski stance	25in	27in	27in	27in	27in	27in
Fuel capacity (US gal)	6.25	6.25	6.25	6.25	6.25	6.25
Track width	15in	15in	15in	15in	18in	18in
Track length	114in	114in	114in	114in	114in	114in
Bore	75mm	59.5mm	64.5mm	67.5mm	76mm	82mm
Stroke	66mm	61mm	61mm	61mm	70mm	73mm
Displacement	291.6cc	339.2cc	393.6cc	436.6cc	635.1cc	771.0cc
Carburetor	1-HD	1-HD	1-HD	2-HD	2-HD	2-HD
Horsepower	20	28	40	38	41	52

The new Ski-Doo T'NT 399 snowmobile had a 399cc engine, 15-inch track, reinforced frame.

enging of the cylinder and higher flow rates. The 400 free air engine produced 40hp at 7500rpm, about 2hp more than the T'NT 440 fan-cooled engine that year.

The T'NT 400's hood lacked the white stripe down the middle and had a large opening below the headlight to allow cooling air directly to the engine. The console on the driver side of the engine was almost wide open to allow for air flow. Only a slide suspension version of the T'NT 400 was built while all other 1972s were available with slide or bogie suspension. The T'NT 400 had chrome-plated skis and shock absorbers on the skis. The T'NT 640 and 775 also got chrome skis for 1972 but were not equipped with shock absorbers. There was a limited number of "Special" 340s and 440s produced with the plated skis and shock absorbers but they were the only T'NT models for 1972 to have ski shocks other than the 400. Mounting the shocks also required the use of a different ski leg, which these machines had.

A new Bombardier patent first appeared on the T'NT 640 and 775 in 1972, for the carbide runners for the skis.

An emergency shut-off switch was mounted on the right handlebar. Only the T'NT models and Blizzard models had this switch in 1972 . The 15in T'NT models had two idler wheels mounted to the outside of the sprockets on both the drive and rear axles to reduce drag at high speed. The 18in T'NT models, the 640 and 775, also had the additional idlers along with the center idler on their axles.

The 640 was fitted with dual Tillotson HD carburetors.

All T'NT models received a cast aluminum chaincase. The 292 and 340 used a double-row, 3/8in pitch chain while the 400, 440, 640, and 775 used a triple-row, 3/8in pitch chain. All T'NT models received manually adjusted, mechanical disk brakes. The driven pulleys were new and mounted a separate, 10in disk (8in on the 292) for the brake. The new driven pulley also utilized a support bearing on the inside end of the shaft. The bearing was attached with a clevice to the handlebar support column and kept the chaincase from twisting under hard acceleration.

the noise level, not increasing horsepower. The 440 was also fitted with a tuned muffler and the late addition, T'NT 400 also got a tuned muffler for 1972.

The T'NT 292 chassis remained virtually unchanged from 1971 but the 340, 400, and 440 received a chassis with a 2in-wider ski stance for a center-to-center distance of 27in, the same stance as the 18in machines.

The T'NT 400 was a low-production sled built with stock class racing in mind. It was powered by an all-new, twin-cylinder, "free air" cooled engine. It utilized the new 28in-stance frame used on the 340 and 440 T'NT models in 1972, and was the first T'NT model to use a free air-cooled engine. The new 399cc engine, or type 398 engine as it was known, was the first vertical twin-cylinder engine used in a T'NT model to break away from the overlapping transfer passage design. The new "perpendicular" layout had been used on the Blizzard engines and certainly prompted its use on the new T'NT engine. The transfer passages were larger and more curved than previous designs and provided better loop scavenging.

The 18in T'NT models along with the 400 T'NT were the first to receive a snow guard as standard equipment. The 292, 340, and 440 did not have a snow guard in 1972. As most 1972 models, the T'NT line received the new "floating" lighting coil.

1973	
★★✔	T'NT F/C
★★★★✔	T'NT F/A

1973

Big things happened in 1973! Ski-Doo's slogan for the year was, "Ski-Doo, the Machine That Changed Winter... Has Changed!" Probably the most startling change to the T'NT for 1973 was the fact that it wasn't yellow and black. There were two series of T'NT models for 1973, the fan-cooled and the free air-cooled models. The fan-cooled models utilized the basic 15in chassis of the previous season. They had new hoods and seats and the hoods and chassis were painted silver. Only a thin, reflective yellow stripe at the base of the hood remained to suggest a connection to Ski-Doo's "standard color." The hood was fiberglass but the louvered, black insert surrounding the headlight was made of polycarbonate plastic and riveted to the hood. An all-new, 293cc engine was added to the 340 and 440 engines already in the line, and the 640 and 775 were dropped. The three silver T'NT models quickly became known as the "silver bullets."

New regulations were imposed on snowmobiles for the 1973 model year, including sound level limits which required the machines to operate within 82dbA at 50ft. This requirement lowered the sound level of a machine by about 40 percent over previous years. The new T'NT models had more tightly enclosed hoods with sound deadening foam on the hoods and consoles, double-wall tuned exhaust systems, and consideration was given to the tolerances of all moving parts on the sleds to minimize sound levels.

The silver bullets were available with slide or bogie suspension. The slide rail suspension was a new, single-rail design. It utilized a shock absorber on the rear arm and, curiously, the rear axle was attached to the tunnel with a link plate on each end. The link plates attached via plastic sliding blocks to allow fore and aft movement of the axle in the plates. Skis on all the T'NT models were equipped with hydraulic shock absorbers, and the rubber ski tip cover, which had first been used on the Blizzard models and in 1972 on the T'NT 400, was standard equipment on all 1973 T'NT models.

The handlebars were padded and equipped with a switch for the new high/low beam headlight on the left and an emergency shut-off switch on the right. The taillight assembly now had a brake light which was powered by a separate brake light coil in the magneto so that its activation would not affect on the intensity of the headlight. The first use of a solid state voltage regulator appeared on the 1973 T'NT models, limiting voltage to 13.5VAC.

While people were discussing whether it was proper or not for Ski-Doo to change from their traditional yellow and black to silver on the T'NT models, out came the T'NT F/A. It was an instant sensation! While the F/As featured a yellow, black, white, and orange color scheme, there seemed to be enough yellow

The Ski-Doo T'NT snowmoblile was available with modification kits for racing enthusiasts.

1973 T'NT models					
	F/C 294	F/C 340	F/C 440	F/A 340	F/A 400
Overall length	99 1/4in	99 1/4in	99 1/4in	99in	99in
Overall width	31 1/2in	31 1/2in	31 1/2in	36in	36in
Approx. weight	370lb	390lb	405lb	385lb	385lb
Ski stance	25.4 in	25.4 in	25.4 in	29.8 in	29.8 in
Fuel capacity	6 US	6 US	6 US	7.2 US	7.2US
Track width	15in	15in	15in	15in	15in
Track length	114in	114in	114in	114in	114in
Bore	27mm	59.5mm	67.5mm	59.5mm	64.5
Stroke	57.5mm	61mm	61mm	61mm	61
Displacement	293.3cc	339.2cc	436.6cc	339.2cc	398.6cc
Carburetor	2-HR	1-HD	1-HD	2-HR	2-HD
Horsepower	24hp	32hp	42hp	45hp	50hp

The 1970 T'NT was available with bogie wheel or, for the first time, slide suspension. The slide rail option was an additional $20.00. *Snow Goer Magazine*

t'nt 400 the newest in the series

Here is the new T'NT 400 model, a free air beauty that is certain to make stock snowmobile racers winners this winter. A new addition to the pulley T'NT line it has twin carbs and a tuned muffler system to deliver a solid 40 hp at 7500 RPM. Styled to look as bad as it runs, the sleek 400 cab directs ample air flow over the engine, has chrome skis, specially calibrated shocks, and a new double action slide suspension all

standard at no extra cost. The air intake silencers and foam lined cab keep noise levels within stock class standards. The 400 has other standard T'NT features like a safety sno-guard, engine shut-off switch, 10" disc brakes, triple link drive chain, aluminium chaincase, and a wide selection of sprockets to choose from. If you are thinking about racing the 400 class, grab a handful of T'NT.

A first for the T'NT line was the 1972 T'NT 400 with its free air-cooled engine. Aimed at stock class competition, the 400 pumped out a solid 40hp. *Tom Halvorson*

and black left on the machine to satisfy the Ski-Doo traditionalists. This new T'NT was a handsome design. Every piece on the machine was new, starting with its all-aluminum frame and belly pan. Even the cross member that supported the ski leg housings was aluminum on the 1973 Free Airs. The frame was the first forward-mount engine design Ski-Doo used in a standard production sled. The Blizzard was the first Ski-Doo to mount the engine ahead of the tunnel in 1972 but it was a limited production race sled.

Two new, free air-cooled Rotax engines with dual Tillotson carburetors were produced for the all-new T'NT models, a 339cc, type 346 engine and a 399cc, type 396 engine. Both were equipped with tapered PTO ends to accept an all-new high-performance clutch. Bombardier had purchased license from Polaris to produce their patented clutch design,

and the Bombardier version was difficult to distinguish from Polaris' own. Its orange color on the outer cover and Bombardier crests on the castings were about the only ways to tell them apart. A lack of understanding of rotational vibrations in the crankshaft at the time led to premature wear in the clutch and many updates were made to the clutch during its use on Ski-Doo. Proper damping of the crankshaft could have greatly improved the clutch's reliability but also would have slowed the F/A's incredible acceleration.

The T'NT F/As were equipped with a jackshaft that mounted the driven pulley on the left end and the chaincase was at the right. Riding on the jackshaft beside the chaincase was a floating brake disk which engaged with a Kelsey-Hayes, H&H Products Division hydraulic caliper. The master cylinder mounted on the handlebar, was entirely plastic, and was produced by H&H products.

The track for the new F/As was a breakthrough in snowmobile track technology. The steel reinforcing rods were replaced by fiberglass rods with a half-round cross section. The rods allowed some flexing of the track without rod breakage, the design was lighter, and the durability of the track was greatly enhanced. The reinforcing rods were referred to as "super resilient rods." This concept in track construction is still used in virtually all snowmobile tracks to this day.

The suspension was entirely new under the Free Airs. The drive sprockets and rear idlers were much larger than had previously been used in production machines, and the link plates at the rear of the suspension were gone. The front arm, or torque arm, trailed while the rear arm led its attachment location in the tunnel. This was the first torque-reacting suspension used on a production Ski-Doo.

The T'NT F/As for 1973 dominated the stock classes they ran in through the 1972-1973 season. There were a number of mechanical problems that presented themselves in the all-new design but the speed, power, and handling were absolutely sensational. It could be clearly seen that the new chassis was a development of the competition department.

Three thousand of each F/A were produced for the 1973 model year. The basic specifications for all the 1973 T'NT models (see specifications box) show the dramatic differences between the F/C and F/A models.

1974

More dramatic changes to the T'NT line were unveiled with the 1974 models. All T'NT models were a front-engine design, electric start T'NT models were offered for the first time, bogie wheels disappeared and all T'NT models rode on torque-reacting, slide rail suspensions, and a long-track model—the T'NT 440 Everest—was added. A 1974 T'NT 440 Everest was the one millionth Ski-Doo produced. That particular Everest is currently on display in the J-Armand Bombardier Museum.

The T'NT models were again divided into two groups for 1974, the free air-cooled models and the fan-cooled models, which included the Everest. The F/As retained the chassis from the previous season, the only significant change being the replacement of the aluminum cross member supporting the ski leg spindle housings with a chrome-moly steel cross member.

The F/Cs received a new frame that mounted the engine ahead of the track tunnel.

The white strip used on the 1972 fan-cooled T'NT models had distributor personnel talking. *Bombardier Ltd.*

1974 Free Air-Cooled T'NT models			
	340	400	440
Overall length	102.5in	102.5in	102.5in
Overall width	36in	36in	36in
Approx. weight	385lb	388lb	391lb
Ski stance	29.8in	29.8in	29.8in
Fuel capacity	6.4 US	6.4US	6.4 US
Track width	15in	15in	15in
Track length	114in	114in	114in
Bore	59.5mm	64.5mm	67.5mm
Stroke	61mm	61mm	61mm
Displacement	339cc	399cc	437cc
Carburetor	2-HR	2-HD	2-HRM
Horsepower	45hp	50hp	55hp

1974 Fan Cooled T'NT models				
	300	340/E	440/E	T'NT Everest
Overall length	100.8in	100.8in	100.8in	105.8in
Overall width	35.5in	35.5in	35.5in	35.5in
Approx. weight	350lb	360/390lb	375/405lb	390lb
Ski stance	28in	28in	28in	28in
Fuel capacity	7.2 US	7.2 US	7.2 US	7.2 US
Track width	16.5in	16.5in	16.5in	16.5in
Track length	114in	114in	114in	124in
Bore	57mm	59.5mm	67.5mm	67.5mm
Stroke	57.5mm	61mm	61mm	61mm
Displacement	293cc	339cc	437cc	437cc
Carburetor	1-HR	1-HD	1-HD	1-HD
Horsepower	25hp	32hp	42hp	42hp

The front section of the frame was steel while the tunnel was aluminum. The T'NT Everest's frame was identical to the T'NT F/C's except that the aluminum tunnel was 5in longer to accommodate its 10in-longer track. All the T'NT F/Cs received a new, 16 1/2in-wide track with fiberglass reinforcing rods. The suspension system was called the torque-reaction slide suspension. It featured two trailing arms, a shock absorber on the rear arm, idler wheels to reduce slider shoe wear, and a new, patented plastic cam adjuster on each of its four springs to allow preload adjustment with the use of the spark plug wrench.

All F/Cs had a chaincase-mounted driven pulley on the left side of the tunnel. The driven pulley mounted a separate brake disk and the caliper was a new, self-adjusting, cable-operated mechanical design. The drive pulley, referred to as the Instant Torque Clutch, was a new square shaft design that transmitted torque from the fixed half to the sliding half by means of a square clutch shaft engaging with a square hole lined with replaceable Teflon coated pads in the sliding half. Two large phenolic rollers, each suspended between two flyweights, transferred centrifugal force to the cam shape of the governor bell. The design was lubrication free and produced a more accurate upshift than the earlier flyweight design operating on a round shaft.

The hoods for the F/Cs were made of Sheet Molded Compound (SMC). The SMC material was a glass fiber, polyester resin mixture that was formed with an inner and outer mold. The process was fast, accurate and produced good finishes on the inside and outside of the hood. It wasn't long into the riding season, however, before the lack of durability of the material showed up. Failure rates were high and a polycarbonate replacement hood was made available under a special warranty for owners who wanted to make the exchange. Consequently, not many of the original hood types exist today.

The F/As had several cosmetic changes for the 1974 model year. The black area on the hood was changed from a semi-gloss black in 1973 to a flat, almost textured black for 1974. A "U" shaped duct that projected

There were two distinct groups of T'NT models for 1973. The fan-cooled models became known as the "silver bullets" and mounted their engines in conventional Ski-Doo fashion on top of the tunnel. *J-A Bombardier Museum*

forward on the hood was added to the large opening in front of the engine. The duct, covered with sound-absorbing foam on the inside, was installed to lower the sound level of the machine. The fuel tank was covered with a textured plastic console that also mounted the instruments. The ski shocks were chrome plated and several details such as elegant cast aluminum caps for the edges of the belly pan were added. The hydraulic brake was replaced with a self-adjusting mechanical brake similar to the one used on the F/C T'NT models. The "ox-horn" handlebar shape introduced on the new F/Cs was added to the F/As along with the new handlebar pad.

A new, 436.6cc, type 436 engine was added to the Free Air line for 1974 and was fitted with two new carburetors from Tillotson, the HRM. All three F/A engine sizes were equipped with Polar Fire ignition and a new 100w lighting coil replaced the 75/23w dual coil arrangement.

The 294 engine had provided a number of problems the previous season. For 1974, the engine was fitted with a new crankshaft design, crankcases, pistons, and a single HR carburetor. The new version of the engine retained the type number, 294, but was called the 300T when used in the 1974 T'NT F/C. The engine proved to be an outstanding engine in its new form. The 340 remained relatively unchanged and was offered in electric or manual start versions. The 437cc engine used in the Everest was a new type 440 Rotax replacing the type 435 Rotax used the previous season. The new engine featured two rear boost ports fed by small windows in the pistons and the cylinder bores were hard chrome-plated rather than fitted with cast iron sleeves. Electric start was not offered on the new Everest model in 1974.

1975

The 300 F/C and 400 F/A were dropped from the 1975 line of T'NT models but a late-season addition, the T'NT 245 RV, provided new excitement.

New hoods graced the Free Airs for 1975. The hood was made longer in front of the engine to allow the duct added the year before to become part of the hood. The headlight was moved down to the right, opposite the air inlet for the free air-cooled engine. The windshield was laid down, barely clearing the top of the handlebars, adding a very streamlined look. The white areas of the previous F/A hood were changed to black and the entire raised center section of the hood was painted orange.

The F/As received a new, aluminum rail suspension system nearly identical to the F/C's. A new self-adjusting, mechanical brake caliper of Bombardier's own design was added and several changes were made to the pulleys. The chokes were removed from the F/C and F/A models and primers were added for quicker starting, particularly in very low temperatures when the engines were harder to pull over. The F/As were fitted with a shaft arrangement that linked the throttles of the twin carbs and allowed use of a single cable without any joints.

The all new T'NT F/As for 1973 had forward-mounted, free air-cooled, 340 and 400cc engines, hydraulic brakes, jackshaft-mounted driven pulleys, high-performance clutches, and a new track with fiberglass reinforcing rods. *J-A Bombardier Museum*

1975	
★★★★★	T'NT R/V
★★★⭒	T'NT F/A
★★★	T'NT F/C
★★★	T'NT 440 Everest/E

T'NT 245 RV	
Overall length	102in
Overall width	41 3/4in
Approx. weight	320lb
Ski stance	34in
Fuel capacity	2.4 US gal
Track width	15in
Track length	105in, 32 cross links
Bore	54mm
Stroke	54mm
Displacement	247cc
Horsepower	43hp @ 7900rpm
Carburetor	Two 34mm Mikuni

The Everest 440 was fitted with Polar Fire CDI for 1975 but the T'NT 440 was not.

The F/Cs and the Everest received new hoods made from polycarbonate plastic and the Everest was made available with electric start. Few other changes were made to the T'NT chassis or their engines. The big show would be put on by the "RV."

The T'NT 245 RV was designed to be a 250 stock class race sled. The bigger F/A T'NT models had been doing very well on the track but the 250 class was being controlled by Arctic Cat. Ski-Doo needed an entry in that class. The entire machine was new and its look was exciting. The chassis was all aluminum with a fiberglass belly pan and the sleek hood was very low. The machine had no windshield and the headlight tucked into the nose cone of the hood beside the cooling air inlet for the free air-cooled engine. The aluminum tunnel was unpainted and the rest of the machine was painted black. Only yellow pinstriping on the hood and a bright orange nose cone highlighted the machine.

Originally a model in the T'NT series, the Everest was introduced in 1974 with its 16.5x124in track. *Bombardier Corp.*

The T'NT 245 R/V was the first "stock" class Ski-Doo to utilize the Bombardier-Rotax central rotary valve engine. *Snow Goer Magazine*

A ski stance of 34in for the RV was the widest of any Ski-Doo to date. The use of a chaincase-mounted driven pulley, rather than a jackshaft arrangement, saved weight and moved the driven pulley toward the center of the machine. The engine mounted almost in the center of the chassis and allowed the RV to fly flat when you just had to get airborne. The belly pan had an opening and small duct that fed cold air directly to the crankcase of the engine. The chaincase on the 1975 T'NT 245 RV was made of magnesium and because the RV was aimed at the race track, it was equipped with a steel-cleated track. Titanium cleats were available as an option and were often used in modified competition. The 15in-wide track was only 105in long and it was the very first internal or involute drive track Bombardier used in production. Rather than the drive sprockets engaging on the cleats, the center band of the track was molded with four rows of rubber lugs and the outer bands had a single row of lugs that engaged with the drive sprockets. This design removed the torque load of the drive axle from the cross links and extended track life. The drive axle was made of aluminum and the drive sprockets or paddles were positioned with set screws on the axle. The track suspension was a shortened version of the torque-reaction system used on the other T'NT models.

Under the hood was the reason for the "RV" moniker, an all-new 247cc, twin-cylinder, free air-cooled, Rotary Valve engine. The central rotary valve, a single rotating valve that controlled intake timing for both cylinders, had been introduced on the Blizzard racers in 1972, but the T'NT 245 RV was the first "production" Ski-Doo to use the design. It was also the first Ski-Doo to use Mikuni VM type, float bowl carburetors. The RV had Polar Fire CDI.

The drive pulley for the RV introduced the latest design of the square shaft clutch. The sliding half was designed to contain the release spring with a hub plug. The spring seat inside the sliding half and the replaceable flat sliders in the hub plug provided the support for the

For 1976, the R/V was focused more for trail use with a windshield, higher mounted headlight, and 15x114in rubber track.

sliding half and the small "heart" diameter of the clutch shaft provided a lower starting ratio.

The RV was a success on the oval racetrack and quickly built a strong following. A 337cc version of the T'NT 245 RV was built as a Moto-Ski model named the Sonic. It was equally successful on the racetrack but didn't have the handsome good looks of the RV. The RV grew into a trail machine in succeeding years and still has a strong following of devoted riders. The superb handling qualities of the RV design were absolutely outstanding and set points of reference for years to come.

1976

The T'NT Free Airs were dropped from the T'NT family and two T'NT RV models, the 250 and 340, were added. There was only one engine size offered in the T'NT F/C, a 340. The 440 was available only in the Everest. Both the T'NT 340 and the T'NT Everest 440 were offered in manual and electric start versions.

There were some "standardization" changes to the T'NT F/C. It received the new, "RV type" drive pulley with hub plug enclosed spring and the longer tunnel and suspension system of the Everest was used to allow installation of the 16 1/2in x124in track. The engine retained its Tillotson HD carburetor but a Mikuni remote fuel pump supplied it. The separate fuel pump helped reduce the chance of vapor lock in the carburetor.

The Everest was still grouped as a T'NT model for 1976 but received a new polycarbonate hood. The black hood had the headlight lowered and offset to the left side. Cooling air entered the hood below the headlight and "Everest" decal to its right, and two louvers at each side of the hood allowed additional air circulation. The engine's fan drew air from the right, upper louver and the heated air from the engine was exhausted out the top of the hood in front of the windshield. The hood was secured by two automatic hood latches at the rear of the hood.

The Everest's five-port engine was fitted with Nikasil-plated rather than hard chrome-plated cylinders for 1976. The Polar Fire ignition was removed from the Everest and replaced with a standard 100w, breaker point magneto.

Late in the 1975-1976 season, the Everest 440 would be joined by a limited production run of the first liquid-cooled Ski-Doo, the T'NT Everest 444 L/C. Liquid cooling was being studied by all the manufacturers at the time as a way to significantly lower sound levels and provide a more stable temperature environment for the increasingly powerful engines.

Interestingly, Ski-Doo's first liquid-cooled engine was spun off a design developed for use in Bombardier's motorcycle line, Can-Am. Bombardier-Rotax and the Can-Am research team in Valcourt, Quebec, had been developing a horizontal twin, central rotary valve, two-stroke cycle, liquid-cooled engine for their proposed street bike, the Can-Am 500. A

number of the engines had been built with six-speed transmissions and were in test in both road race and street trim. *Cycle* magazine was given the opportunity to test one of the prototypes and ended up giving the machine the magazine cover and the headline, "Can-Am's Unbelievable 330-pound, Z-1 Eater." The Kawasaki Z-1 was a four-cylinder, 900cc king of the road at the time.

Legislators were considering placing emission controls on motorcycles at the time, which would have—and eventually did—put an end to two-stroke cycle street bikes in the United States. A decision had to be made by Bombardier whether or not to proceed with the street bike project. It was decided to discontinue development of the street bike but the dies used to make the twin Siamese cylinders and cylinder head were used to produce the top end for Ski-Doo's first liquid-cooled production engine, the type 444.

The cylinders were in a horizontal position on the motorcycle but when standing vertically on a snowmobile crankcase, the name "Bombardier" on the sides of the cylinders and head read from bottom to top on one side and top to bottom on the other. The cylinder head of the original 444 had a water jacket around the perimeter of the head but the combustion chamber domes were finned. When the cylinders laid horizontally in the

A 340cc version of the R/V was built as a Moto-Ski. The Sonic was as successful on the racetrack as the R/V but lacked the R/V's sleek styling. *Patrick K. Snook*

motorcycle, the combustion chamber fins were presented directly to the air flow but when standing nearly vertically in the snowmobile, the domes of the cylinder heads did not cool adequately, which eventually led to a redesign of the head.

The crankcase for the new engine ran the rotary valve shaft through to the front of the engine, where a centrifugal water pump was mounted at its end. Water passages to the cylinders were routed through the front of the crankcase, and coolant was collected in the head, controlled by a thermostat and fed to the tunnel-mounted, extruded aluminum heat exchangers. The 444 produced about 50hp at 6700rpm. The engine was fitted with a double-wall tuned muffler and a single 34mm Mikuni carburetor.

The hood was the same shape as the new Everest 440 hood but was yellow. The machine had a rear view mirror on the left side of the hood, electric handlebar heaters, electric starter, and a flashy seat with yellow and black plaid cover and black sides.

The T'NT RVs for 1976 were repositioned from stock class race sleds to high-performance trail sleds. The tunnels and suspension system were stretched an additional 5in to accept a standard 15x114in rubber track. The belly pan was made higher to provide more room under the hood and the hood itself was made higher. The headlight was moved from the opening in the nose cone to the top of the hood, just below the windshield. The nose cone was opened all the way across to allow cooling air to the engine and the exhaust system. An aluminum chaincase replaced the magnesium version of the previous year.

A modified racing kit was available for both the 250 and 340 RV, and it included a smaller diameter, lower inertia magneto, twin tuned exhaust pipes, longer duration rotary valve, Nikasil-plated cylinders with longer port durations, and clutch parts with the proper calibration for the kit. A cleated track kit was also available for the all out racer.

1977		
★★★★		T'NT R/VCC
★★		T'NT R/V
★★★		T'NT 340 F/A
★★		T'NT 440 F/A
★★★↓		T'NT F/C

1977

Separated from the T'NT family in 1977, the Everest would continue as a separate series through the 1983 model year. The T'NT had a new, all-steel chassis for 1977 and was offered with free air-cooled 340 and 440 engines and a fan-cooled 440 engine. No electric start models were offered. The hoods were a new look for Ski-Doo and were often referred to as the "cube" look hood. At an overall length of 100in, the new chassis was almost 6in shorter than the previous T'NT chassis. The chassis was widened to 36.3in, the width of the Everest chassis, and fitted with the 16 1/2x114in track. The ski stance remained at 28in. Approximate weight of the 340 was 400lb while the two 440s came in at about 405lb.

The two free air-cooled engines shared the same 61mm stroke bottom end. Both were equipped with a single VM 34 Mikuni carburetor and a single tuned muffler. The type 440, fan-cooled engine was produced with both Nikasil-plated cylinder bores and cast iron-lined cylinders. Early production models were equipped with the Nikasil cylinders. As they were phased out of production on the 440, the cast iron-lined cylinders took over. All three engines were fitted with breaker point magnetos, a two-roller, square shaft clutch and the driven pulley was chaincase mounted.

The 440 F/A T'NT had many engine

GIANT KILLER

Had it been built, Can-Am's 500cc two-stroke street twin would have made existing cafe racers as absolute as the suicide clutch.
by Tony Murphy

Bombardier was testing a motorcycle design in the mid-seventies that utilized a central rotary valve, liquid-cooled engine. In the motorcycle, the cylinders mounted in a horizontal configuration. *Cycle Magazine*

problems during the season and a number of modifications were factory authorized.

Only a 340 R/V was produced for 1977 with an air-cooled engine. The chassis and engine remained relatively unchanged from 1976 but the engine was fitted with two tuned pipes emptying into a single after muffler, a design employed to this day on high-performance models. The R/V was never referred to as a T'NT for 1977. The large T'NT decal that graced the hood the previous year was replaced with a large R/V decal. For the purpose of this book, however, I will include it in the T'NT family.

An exciting, limited-production version of the R/V was introduced as a 1977 model, the R/V Cross Country. The chassis was nearly identical to the standard R/V's but used a 4130 chrome-moly steel front cross member rather than aluminum, and heat exchangers were mounted through both vertical sides of the tunnel. The seat was equipped with an additional fuel tank at the rear. The engine was a magnificent, all-new, type 354, liquid-cooled, rotary valve twin that made around 75hp. The engine ran a new, six-pole CDI system from Bosch. The magneto was "inside out" compared to the conventional Rotax layout. The magnet-flywheel

mounted in against the main bearing and the stator plate mounted to an aluminum plate fastened to the crankcase. An additional damper-flywheel held the starter cup and mounted on a spline or taper, both types were made on the end of the crankshaft. The cylinders were Nikasil-plated and had a single exhaust port. Cylinders were separate castings but the cylinder head was a single casting that joined the cylinders and collected the coolant from both of them. The engine was fitted with twin tuned expansion chambers and two Mikuni VM 38 carburetors.

The drive pulley or clutch was a new design. It was a square shaft type but utilized two replaceable ramps that could be custom shaped for different shifting characteristics. The design made the clutch much more tunable. The 354's power curve was rather narrow and the clutch set-up had to be spot on for peak performance.

The RVCC, as it became known, was extremely fast and heralded many new things to come from Ski-Doo!

The cylinder and head from the prototype Can-Am was mounted on a snowmobile crankcase and first used to power the limited production run of the T'NT Everest 444 LC in 1976. The engine shown here is a modified version of the 444 used in the 1976 Ski-Doo Sno-Pro race sleds. *Lance Parthe*

1978

For 1978, the troublesome 440 FA was dropped and the 340 FA and 440 FC returned. Other than some color and decal changes, the T'NT models remained virtually unchanged from their equals of the previous season.

The R/V also returned almost unchanged from 1977. It was to be the final year for the R/V but its incredible handling chassis would live on in the 1978 and 1979 model years as a Blizzard model. Ski-Doo's introduction of the incredibly fast RVCC the year before got the

racing associations thinking about horsepower rather than displacement limits as a means of classifying sleds. A limit of 45hp, plus or minus 10 percent, was selected as the allowable limit for cross country racing. The 354 almost made that much power with one cylinder! There was no way the 354 could be used in competition. The R/V Cross Country sled for 1978 used the air-cooled, type 345 engine fitted with the Nikasil cylinders and heads from the 1976 modified kit. A single tuned muffler was fitted on the engine and it dropped the combination into the new horsepower limit. Two hundred and fifty of these RVCCs were produced.

The machine was incredible in snow and the perfect balance of the R/V chassis and its light weight allowed the machine to dominate cross-country racing for years. Of course it didn't hurt to have Gerard Karpik piloting

For the 1977 model year, the Everest began its own series and left the T'NT line-up. Shown here is the 1977 Everest 444 LC. *Bombardier Corp.*

and Gerard and brother Randy tuning! The combination continued winning against stronger and stronger competition all the way through the winter of 1980 on that same, incredible little R/V.

The T'NT model line ended in 1978 with the T'NT 340 FA and the T'NT 440 FC. In its wake were some monumental advances in snowmobile technology and thousands of wins on the oval and cross country race tracks. Many concepts first presented on the T'NT models live on today. Eleven years of T'NT models produced a lot of "Firsts"!

An all-new 1977 T'NT series included two free-air models, the T'NT 440 (next page top) and F/A 340, and one fan-cooled model, the F/C 440 (above). Free-air hoods are black on top and front with yellow side panels highlighted by black stripes. The fan-cooled model has a yellow hood trimmed in black. *Bombardier Corp.*

One of three liquid-cooled models produced by Bombardier for the 1977 model year was the incredibly fast, RV 340 Cross Country. *Bombardier Corp.*

For 1978, the cross country version of the R/V was equipped with a free air-cooled engine and special kit to meet new ICCSF racing specifications. With Gerard Karpik aboard, the R/V dominated cross country racing for years. *Bombardier Corp.*

Chapter 6

The Nordic

1969 Nordic	
Overall length	97in
Overall width	33 3/4in
Approx. weight	360lb/400lb(Electric)
Ski stance	27in
Fuel capacity	6.25 gal US
Track width	18in
Track length	114in
Bore	62mm
Stroke	61mm
Displacement	368cc
Carburetor	1 Tillotson HR
Horsepower	22hp

1969

The introduction of the Nordic signaled the beginning of sophistication in snowmobile design. Perhaps no other snowmobile de-

This curious, early photo shows a 1969 Nordic running with a 399 T'NT. Could there be a 669 engine under the hood and only later was the chassis painted black and a new hood design given the 669 T'NT for 1969? *Bombardier Ltd.*

sign was more copied by the competition than was the 1969 Nordic. Some competitor's versions were so close only the color identified them as something other than a Ski-Doo!

The Nordic chassis was shared with the wide-track, 18in T'NT models but it was painted yellow while the T'NT's chassis was painted black. The all-steel chassis incorporated a cross member that rose up over the plastic fuel tank to support the ski legs. The belly pan wrapped up the sides to the level of the seat and a chrome-plated bumper covered the joint line of the hinged, fiberglass hood. The hood had a retractable headlight and a safety break-away windshield.

Suspension for the new Nordic was Ski-Doo's classic, flexible bogie system. The backrest and rear storage compartment was also made of polycarbonate plastic and housed the battery for the electric start version of the Nordic. The tunnel-mounted engine was enclosed with a console. The console mounted the optional speedometer and tachometer. The electric start version was even equipped with a cigarette lighter.

Only one engine was offered in the original Nordic, a 368cc, type 371 engine making 22hp. The engine was one of the new breed of vertical twin-cylinder engines designed by Rotax expressly for use in Ski-Doos. The muffler was the typical "can" used at the time and was not tuned. Exhaust from the muffler was dumped out in the center of the chassis just ahead of the track.

1971
★★↘
★★★
Nordic 399, 640
Scandic

1970				
★★↘		Nordic 399		
★★★		Nordic 640		

1970

There were three Nordic models for 1970; the 371 engine was replaced by a 399 offered in manual and electric start and a new 640 electric start version joined them. The chassis for the Nordic models was painted black and a new, polycarbonate plastic hood with louvers at each side replaced the fiberglass hood of the previous season. It was the first time a material other than fiberglass or steel had been used as a hood material on a Ski-Doo or probably any other snowmobile. Little else changed on the Nordic models for 1970.

Basic engine specifications for the 1970 Nordic models were as follows:

	399	640
Bore	64.5mm	76mm
Stroke	61mm	70mm
Displacement	399cc	635cc
Carburetor	1 Tillotson HR	1 Tillotson HD
Horsepower	24hp	35hp

1971

For 1971, the black decals in the hood vents were removed, leaving the hood entirely yellow. A front grab handle or bumper was added and the stirrups were changed from a tubular design to a stronger tapered design. The skis were entirely new. Their cross section was square, offering a stronger ski and more positive steering in snow. A new, deep-profile track, which was added to all models for 1971, provided 20 percent greater traction. The chaincase received a spring-loaded tensioner to replace the earlier eccentric adjuster.

The 399 and 640 Nordic models were available with or without electric starter and, for the first time and for an extra $20.00, with or without slide suspension.

A derivative model of the Nordic, the Scandic was first produced as a 1971 model. It was a bare bones 18in chassis powered by a single-cylinder, type 337 engine that displaced 335cc and produced 20hp. The new model weighed 335lb, 25lb less than the lightest Nordic. The Scandic had no console or storage space in its relocatable backrest. The fiberglass hood had a fixed position headlight. Scandic was available only with bogie suspension and manual start. Scandic was intended to be a utility sled with superb deep snow capability, and was priced to retail at only $945.00.

1972		
★★↘		Nordic 440
★★★		Nordic 640 ER

1972

A major change occurred on the 1972 640 Nordic... it was black! The entire machine

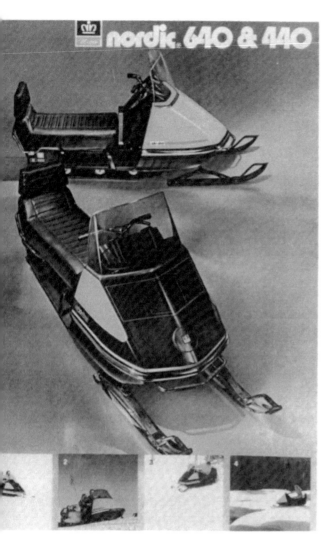

nordic. 640 & 440

	1972 Nordic	
	440/E	**640ER**
Overall Length	101in	101in
Overall width	34.5in	34.5in
Approx. weight	405lb/440lb	474lb
Ski stance	27in	27in
Fuel capacity	6.9 US gal	6.9 US gal
Track width	18in	18in
Track length	114in	114in
Bore	67.5mm	76mm
Stroke	61mm	70mm
Displacement	437cc	635cc
Carburetor	1 Tillotson HR	1 Tillotson HD
Horsepower	28hp	35hp

The 1972 Nordic 640 was the first Ski-Doo not to use yellow as its dominant color. The all-black Nordic was an elegant-looking machine with just enough yellow trim on its hood to make the Ski-Doo connection. *J-A Bombardier Museum*

was black, and only a yellow stripe on the sides of the hood and quite large yellow panels above the stripes identified it as a Ski-Doo. The 440, which replaced the 399 in 1972, had a black frame with a more conventional, yellow hood.

Almost everything was new on the 1972 Nordic models. The frame was entirely new with a more pointed nose, and because the new backrest had no storage space in it, the top of the tunnel had a storage compartment built in. The new seat was hinged on its right side to gain access to the space beneath. All the Nordic models for 1972 were fitted with cast-aluminum chaincases and the 640 also got reverse. All 640s were equipped with electric start while the 440 was built with and without the convienient feature. Slide or bogie suspension was available on all models. The new chaincase mounted a driven pulley with separate disk for the new mechanical disk brake.

A new "floating" lighting coil allowed the use of a full wave rectifier and greatly increased the charging capacity on the electric start models. The 1972 Nordic models were the first Ski-Doos to be equipped with a high/low beam headlight. Both electric and manual start models had the feature. The 440 engine used in the Nordic for 1972 was the type 434, which produced 28hp versus the T'NT's type 435, which produced about 38hp.

No changes were made to the Scandic model for 1972, as it remained an extension of the 1971 production.

1973	
★★★	Nordic 640 ER
★★	Scandic

1973

The all-black Nordic 640 of the previous year seemed pretty tame compared to the all-brown Nordic 640 for 1973. The machine remained relatively unchanged from 1972 but the rich brown color was a shocker for Ski-Doo traditionalists. The skis and their shock absorbers were chrome-plated for a real touch of class. It was the first time shocks were used on a Nordic model. A speedometer and tachometer were always standard equipment on the 640 Nordic models but for 1973, a modular instrument assembly included an electric fuel gauge. The gauge required a sending unit mounted in the fuel tank. A new, slightly smaller, 6.4 US gallon tank, was designed to accept the sending unit for the convenient new feature. A brake light and emergency engine shut-off switch were added, as were acoustical foam inside the hood and a new intake silencer to meet new sound level limits imposed in 1973. The 640 ER was the only Nordic model produced for 1973 and was only available with bogie wheel suspension.

An interesting exhaust system appeared on the 1973 640 Nordic, the snow-cooled muffler. The new sound level limits required tighter enclosure of the engine compartment, which resulted in higher underhood temperatures and a need for quieter mufflers. Ski-Doo engineers came up with a clever design to address both concerns. The basic muffler was enclosed with a second jacket that covered the top and sides of the muffler but was open at the bottom where it was sealed to the chassis with a flexible coupling. Underneath, the jacket was exposed to the high-pressure air flow that exists at the front of the tunnel when the machine is in operation. The double jacket around the muffler lowered the radiated sound and the snow and air mixture flowing between the muffler and the jacket lowered underhood temperatures.

A new system in drive pulley lubrication was tried on the 1973 Nordic. It was called the "Lubri-matic System." The PTO end of the crankshaft was drilled through the lobe of the crankshaft. A second hole was drilled perpendicular to the drilled crankshaft end. The clutch shaft had a hollow center which had a small hole drilled perpendicular to it. Centrifugally separated engine lubricating oil could make its way into the clutch shaft and flow out onto the shaft's surface, lubricating the sliding half's bushing.

For 1973, the Scandic was put on a version of the new Nordic chassis. The sheet metal chaincase with drum brake remained from the previous chassis. A new fiberglass hood with fixed headlight covered its 335cc, single-cylinder engine, and a console was installed behind the engine to meet the new sound level limits.

1974	
★★★	Nordic 640 ER

1974

It was the final year for the 18in track Nordic 640ER and few changes were implemented. Problems in plating and polishing of the chrome ski resulted in a removable grab handle on the ski tip so they could be polished individually. The feature-laden Nordic bowed out wearing the rich brown finish of the 1973 season. It was the year of Ski-Doo's one millionth machine, and, fittingly, it was the Everest that would continue the innovation and style that the Nordic pioneered.

There were no Scandic models produced for the 1974 model year but the Nordic, to be spelled Nordik, and the Scandic would return on a modified Citation chassis in the eighties. Their story is continued in the Citation chapter (chapter 11).

The 1972 Ski-Doo Nordic 640 had reverse, electric
start, and cigarette lighter all standard, it was the luxury
model for the sophisticated snowmobile consumer.
J-A Bombardier Museum

For 1973 the Nordic was used for more color experimentation. Finished in a rich brown color, the Nordic was available only with a 640 engine. Reverse gear and electric start were standard equipment. *Bombardier Corp.*

Chapter 7

The Blizzard

1970 ★★★★	Blizzard (all models)

1970

Rumors about a series of race sleds started flying after the West Yellowstone Round-Up in March of 1969. The West Yellowstone event was used by the manufacturers to test many concepts being considered for the coming season. Bombardier's factory race team absolutely cleaned house at the event using several new Rotax racing engines and a number of components that the informed knew were not current production items. When the snowmobile press spread the word of Ski-Doo's dominance at Yellowstone, every Ski-Doo racer in North America, and a few in Europe, clamored to get their hands on one of the new machines!

As late as the end of July in 1969, the Blizzard was still a rumor to everyone outside Valcourt. A July 29, 1969, letter from Steve Ave, two-time Eagle River World Champion and Director of Parts and Service for Halvorson Equipment, a Ski-Doo distributor in Duluth, Minnesota, addressed their dealer network:

"Dear Dealer:

"There has been much speculation and rumor concerning special race machines for this season. To set the record straight, to the

The 1970 Blizzard 292 and 340 raised quite a stir and dominated stock class racing when they were fitted with the first tuned muffler used on a Ski-Doo to make them legal in the stock events. *Doug Hayes*

best of our knowledge, there are supposed to be some highly sophisticated racing machines that will be manufactured by Bombardier. They have been called the 'Blizzard Series' by the rumor mill up to this point.

"We at Halvorson Equipment believe and hope that things like the 292 rotary valve, 340, 440, etc. will become a reality, however, these units would be in very short supply. A dealer will not automatically receive any of these units. If and when they become available,

1970 Blizzard models

	292	340	436	636	776
Overall length	98in	98in	98in	98in	98in
Overall width	30in	30in	34in	34in	34in
Approx. weight	285lb	285lb	365lb	375lb	375lb
Ski stance	24in	24in	27in	27in	27in
Fuel capacity (US gal)	3.5	3.5	6.25	6.25	6.25
Track width	15in	15in	18in	18in	18in
Track length	114in	114in	114in	114in	114in
Bore	75mm	78mm	67mm	76mm	82 mm
Stroke	66mm	70mm	61mm	70mm	73 mm
Displacement	291.6cc	334.5cc	429.9cc	635.1cc	771.0
Carburetor	1-HD	1-HD	2-HR	2-HD	2-HD
Horsepower	28hp	32hp	45hp	64hp	82hp

The Blizzard models saw their first official competition in the fall of 1969 at the indoor race in Duluth, Minnesota. Here the Ski-Doo winners for the day line up behind a dirty 1970 Blizzard 776.

Slide rail suspension was standard for the Blizzard but bogie wheels were picked for the sticky Duluth race. *Basgen Photography*

Three cylinder designs were used in the 650 and 800 class Blizzard models for 1971. *Jack Reichert*

they will go to the people who can best fulfill their intended use.

"If you, as a dealer, sincerely believe you have someone who is honestly qualified to compete with one of these vehicles, you may make a request for one by mail only to the Racing Department, Halvorson Equipment, Inc."

A 1970 sales brochure for the T'NT models included a line drawing of the Blizzard with this note: "And when you're at snowmobile meets this winter, look out for the Blizzard. It's a new concept in racing machines built to keep us on the winning track. Strictly a limited production racer, the Blizzard is recommended for registered racing circuit drivers."

A company jointly owned by Doug Dehnert, John Staver, and Bombardier, Ltd., named "Doug's Incorporated" and located in Virginia, Minnesota, produced high-performance parts exclusively for Ski-Doo. At the formal opening of the facility, Laurent Beaudoin, president of Bombardier, Ltd., noted on

October 17, 1969, that "Deliveries [of Blizzard models] will begin in two weeks starting with the 776 and descending through each class."

A month later a memo discussing production of the Blizzard 292 and 340 was sent by Jean-Paul Groulx to all Ski-Doo distributors.

"Please be advised that we are planning to produce the required 100 units of each of the types listed above on Saturday, the 22nd of November, 1969. These units will be distributed the following week across North America so that they will be in the hands of dealers in required quantities before the 1st of December deadline. Because of the speed needed to distribute these units, you may not have all of them in your territory by December 1, 1969. However, be assured that 100 will be available at retail, a fact which can be verified if any association wants to question us on the subject."

The Blizzard models were initially visualized as only competing in the modified classes. The fact that the 292 and 340 could be pro-

duced in time and in the quantity needed to meet the regulating body's rules meant they could be raced in the stock classes *if* they had a muffler to replace their standard, unsilenced expansion chamber. Doug Dehnert of Doug's Inc. put together what turned out to be the first tuned muffler used on a Ski-Doo. It was a megaphone enclosed in a canister with a separate tail pipe of a tuned length. The whole assembly fit onto the exhaust flange on the cylinder and exhausted out behind the hood by the driver's right foot. The muffler was not quiet by today's standards but was much quieter than the expansion chamber and produced quite good power and a very pleasant exhaust tone.

The 1970 Blizzard 292 and 340 went on to dominate their stock classes for several seasons as well as compete in the modified classes.

The 1970 Blizzard models were based on the 15in and 18in T'NT models. The 292 and 340 engine sizes utilized the 15in chassis and track while the 440, 640 and 776 were mount-

The 250cc Elan Blizzard was one of the cutest sleds ever to hit the race track during the 1971 season. The black-and-white checkered "racing tape" used on the 1971 Blizzard models became one of the hottest selling accessories for the season. *Jack Reichert*

The first time people in the Midwest saw the front-engine Blizzard for 1972 was at a drag race in the summer of 1971. The author gobbled up the competition with this alcohol-burning 797. *Basgen Photography*

ed on the 18in, all steel chassis. All five models rode on Ski-Doo's jointed slide rail system. The 15in chassis utilized an aluminum frame with steel front cross member to provide support for the ski leg housings. This allowed the use of a separate plastic fuel tank in the machine along with a replaceable belly pan.

Bombardier had been experimenting with polycarbonate plastic in a number of areas and was impressed with its low temperature stability and extremely high impact resistance. The 1970 Nordic and Ski-Boose would receive polycarbonate hoods. It was decided to make the belly pan for the 15in and 18in Blizzard models out of the incredible new plastic. The 15in mod-

els had a yellow pan and the 18in models had a black pan. The material worked well in limited tests but after a few races, fuel tanks were falling through the belly pan!

Some quick testing revealed the plastic's aversion to aromatic solvents. Spilled gasoline, cleaning solvents, and the non-gasoline fuels some of us were experimenting with could turn the polycarbonate belly pans to dust. Bombardier quickly replaced the pans with pans made of fiberglass. Very few 1970 Blizzard models exist with the original belly pan intact.

The Blizzard hoods were the basic shape of the T'NT hoods for 1970 with large air scoops in the front and ducts added inside to

Andre Bombardier, at the time VP, research and development for Bombardier Limited's Ski-Doo Division, points out the new central rotary valve location on the radically new engine used in the Blizzard 400 and 440 for 1972. *Bombardier Ltd.*

focus the air directly on the free air-cooled engines. The windshields were low and they had no headlight or taillights. The only wiring on the machines was the new Bosch, breakerless CDI, a kill switch mounted on the reinforced handlebar, and a wire to the standard tachometer. The CDI was a first for Ski-Doo and was used on all five Blizzard engines.

The CDI system made by Bosch for Rotax was actually quite advanced. It used one trigger or pulse coil per cylinder as well as a separate timing circuit for each cylinder on the twins. Only the charging circuit and condenser was shared by the cylinders. One pulse per cylinder per revolution was generated and the trigger circuit even had reverse rotation protection designed in. The breakerless design and high charging capacity meant stable spark, even at very high rpms. There was only one problem with the new ignition system... it failed about 80 percent of the time! Charging coils and solid state components in the trigger boxes were failing at very high rates and a standard breaker point magneto was supplied to replace them in the field while Bosch and Rotax worked out the component problems.

The driveline for the Blizzard was pretty standard fair. A sheet metal chaincase mounted the cam action driven pulley but the chaincase used a spring loaded automatic chain tensioner rather than the traditional eccentric cam tensioner. A standard, drum-type driven pulley was used but a mechanical disk brake caliper was used rather than a shoe against the drum found on other models. The drive pulley was the standard four-flyweight design found on all Ski-Doos but reinforced to handle the additional power of the new engines.

All five engines were totally new for the Blizzard line. They were free air-cooled, piston port designs fitted with one Tillotson carburetor per cylinder and one tuned expansion chamber per cylinder. The 292 and 340 were single-cylinder engines and shared a common crankcase. The 292 used a 66mm stroke crankshaft while the 340 had a 70mm stroke crank. The cylinders were cast aluminum, sleeved with cast iron liners. Cooling fins on both the cylinders and the heads were enormous, giving the engines a large appearence and excellent cooling. When using methanol as a fuel, the fins had to be cut down to get the engine up to an acceptable operating temperature. The intake port sloped down toward the crankcase mounting the carburetor at a 30 degree angle. The exhaust port also exited the cylinder at a 30 degree downward angle.

A center line connecting the exhaust and intake ports was perpendicular to the crankshaft on all the Blizzard engines. This allowed for better flow through the cylinder, though it did make the twin-cylinder engines physically longer. The 440 was a piston port twin with rather unusual trench type combustion chambers in the cylinder heads. The 440 utilized its own crankcase while the twin-cylinder 640 and 776 used the same crankcase with different stroke crankshafts. The crankshafts on all the Blizzard engines were a full circle design with tapered crank lobes that fit very tightly with the crankcase. The crankcase was "stuffed" from Rotax, even the connecting rods were polished on the Blizzard engines.

The coils, trigger boxes, and condenser for the ignition system on the twins mounted in a cast aluminum box on the front of the crankcase. The box was covered with a black

1971 Blizzard models							
	246	291	336	397	437	645	797
Overall length	88.5in	98in	98in	98in	98in	98in	98in
Overall width	29.5in	30.6in	30.6in	30.6in	30.6in	34in	34in
Approx. weight	246lb	328lb	328lb	351lb	351	420lb	420lb
Ski stance	23in	24in	24in	24in	24in	27in	27in
Fuel cap. (US gal)	6.25	6.25	6.25	6.25	6.25	9.6	9.6
Track width	15in	15in	15in	15in	15in	16 1/2in	16 1/2in
Track length	114in	114in	114in	114in	114in	114in	114in
Bore (mm)	69.0	75.0	78.5	64.5	67.5	67	74.5
Stroke (mm)	66	66	70	61	61	61	61
Displacement	246cc	291.6cc	338.8cc	398.4cc	436.4cc	645.2cc	797.7cc
Carburetor	1 HD	1 HD	1 HD	2 HD	2 HD	3 HD	3 HD
Horsepower	29hp	31hp	36hp	42hp	45hp	71hp	88hp

plastic cover. All Blizzard pistons had Teflon coated domes, a rectangular ring and an "L" ring at the top.

1971
★★★★   Blizzard 250
★★★   Blizard 295, 340, 400, 440
★★★★   Blizzard 640, 797

while the standard Élan used a single row, 1/2in pitch chain. A Blizzard-look hood with large air inlet and a snow flap were about the only other things to separate the machine from a standard Élan. The 246cc free air engine pumped out about 24hp and that made the 246lb machine a absolute kick to drive!

The other Blizzard models were put on new chassis and suspensions for 1971. The 292, 340, the new 400, and the 440 were built on an aluminum, 15in chassis which bor-

1971

The 1971 Blizzard models were restricted to the modified classes but the 1970, 292, and 340, with muffler, were still allowed in their respective stock classes and they continued to dominate during the 1970-1971 season. Two engine sizes were added to the 1971 Blizzard line. A 400cc limit was placed on the Winnipeg to Saint Paul 500-mile cross country race. A sleeved-down version of the 440 engine filled the order. In Europe and in some local events, the 250cc class was still holding interest. A free air-cooled, 246cc engine was built and installed in a slightly modified version of the Élan's steel chassis. Though officially known as the Blizzard 246, the new little race sled was unofficially known as the Élan-Blizzard.

The Blizzard 246 used the Élan's standard track and bogie wheel suspension. The Élan was equipped with a pivoting arm brake but the Blizzard 246 had a chaincase that used the drum brake and double row, 3/8in pitch chain

The 1972 Blizzard 797 and 640 remained relatively unchanged for 1973 with changes made only to the clutch and carburetors and the addition of an orange panel in front of the engine. *Basgen Photography*

91

rowed from the new Olympique chassis for 1971. The three-cylinder 640 and 797 engines got a new, aluminum 16 1/2in chassis. All the Blizzard models were available with a steel-cleated or all-rubber track. Chaincases were cast aluminum and the driven pulley was equipped with a separate brake disk for the cable operated brake caliper. The 640 and 797 driven pulleys were equipped with an additional support bearing that fastened with a clevis to the steering support column. The drive pulleys were new for all the Blizzard models. The new design allowed for very high clutch engagement speeds utilizing four flyweights whose center of gravity in relation to its pivot point could be carefully adjusted. The shaft on the clutch was splined to transmit torque from the inner to the outer half, leaving the weights free to handle the shifting operation.

The suspension still utilized a jointed rail but the rear axle was mounted on the rails rather than link plates. The link plates were still there but fastened via sliding plastic blocks on the ends of the rear axle.

The single- and twin-cylinder engines were all fitted with an updated version of the Bosch CDI. The 640 and 797, which were three-cylinder engines for 1971, used a breaker point ignition with three generating coils and three sets of points and condensers. All engines were equipped with one carburetor and one tuned pipe per cylinder.

The 295, 340, and 440 Blizzard models for 1973 had a totally new look based on the T'NT F/As of the year. All three models utilized the new rotary valve engine design. *Bombardier Corp.*

1972	
★★★★↙	**Blizzard (all models)**

1972

The way Bombardier was producing all-new designs powered by all-new engines season after season was almost unbelievable. 1972 was no different when a new line of Blizzard models sporting completely new engines was introduced. Six engine sizes were used on the same 15in aluminum chassis. The engine mounted low, in front of the tunnel for

the first time on a Ski-Doo. The chassis had indestructible, 1in diameter, forged steel ski legs at a wide 29 3/4in stance. A short, aluminum chaincase joined the jackshaft with the drive axle on the right side of the machine. The jackshaft was mounted in a cast-aluminum pillow block with dual ball bearings on the left end of the shaft next to the driven pulley. On the chaincase end of the shaft, a floating brake disk engaged with a Kelsey-Hayes hydraulic brake caliper that was mounted on the pillow block. The driven pulley had stamped aluminum sheaves for the first time.

All the Blizzard models were equipped with a steel-cleated track. The drive sprockets engaged the steel cleats to drive the track. The suspension used extruded aluminum, single-piece rails and all the suspension components were made of aluminum. The suspension system was 35 percent lighter than the previous year's. The chrome-plated shocks on the skis were adjustable with three different compression damping rate positions.

The hood for the new Blizzard models was a clever, two-piece design that was used on all the Blizzard models. The main hood was identical on all models but a hinged in-

1972 Blizzard models

	293	340	395	438	645	797
Overall length	102in	102in	102in	102in	102in	102in
Overall width	36in	36in	36in	36in	36in	36in
Approx. weight	390lb	390lb	380lb	380lb	415lb	415lb
Ski stance	29 3/4in	29 3/4in	29 3/4in	29 3/4in	29 3/4in	29 3/4in
Fuel cap. (US gal)	6.5	6.5	6.5	6.5	6.5	6.5
Track width	15in	15in	15in	15in	15in	15in
Track length	120in	120in	120in	120in	120in	120in
Bore	50mm	53.3mm	64.5mm	67.5mm	67mm	74.5mm
Stroke	50mm	50mm	61mm	61mm	61mm	61mm
Displacement	294.5cc	337.2cc	398.4cc	436.4cc	645.2cc	797.7cc
Carburetor	3-HR	3-HR	2-HD	2-HD	3 HD	3 HD
Horsepower	42hp	48hp	60hp	67hp	85hp	102hp

sert in front of the engine could be changed to work with the twin- or triple-cylinder engines. The hood had no windshield.

Power for the Blizzard models was as exciting as the new chassis. The 293, 340, 645, and 797 were all three-cylinder designs. The 645 and 797 were not reworked versions of the 1971 Blizzard's, they were completely new! The 395 and 438 were twin-cylinder, central rotary valve designs. Steve Ave's letter of July 29, 1969, to the Halvorson dealers had suggested Rotax was working with rotary valve designs but this was the first rotary valve engine used in a production sled. All the new engines were free air-cooled and had one carburetor and one tuned expansion chamber per cylinder.

The 293 and 340 triples were interesting engines with personalities of their own. They sounded wonderful, and they made good peak power, but they were heavy, and their high rotating mass made them slow accelerating. Rotax used an external labyrinth seal between cylinders rather than a rubber seal or internal labyrinth. The design produced a rather large area to seal dynamically between the cylinders. At cranking speeds it was difficult to create the turbulence at the seal to allow proper pressure rises in the crankcase for proper transfer to the cylinder. Once the engine started, it ran and idled fine but starting could be a bear, especially when the engine was warm and the case had expanded a bit, increasing the clearance at the labyrinth seal. The smaller the pumping volume of the cylinder, the more difficult starting became. Race drivers often fitted the 293 with a "V"

belt pulley on the flywheel and removed the recoil starter. A chainsaw motor also fitted with a pulley was then used to crank the 293 with a belt.

The rotary valve twins were extremely dependable, easy starting, and produced a wide power band. Yvon Duhamel won the 1972 International 500 mile Winnipeg to St. Paul cross country race aboard a 1972 395 Blizzard, rotary valve twin. The 797 for 1972 was the first "stock" engine to top the 100hp mark.

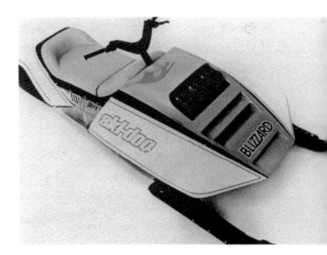

Perhaps the best styled race sled ever built was the 1974 Blizzard. Due to the energy shortage of the day, Bombardier decided to drop out of competition for the year, and the sled was never seen on the racetracks. *Bombardier Ltd.*

The drive pulley used a round shaft with no splines. At the end of the shaft, two flats were machined. These flats engaged with matching flats in the governor cup and transferred torque to the sliding half of the pulley via plastic buttons on the arms of the cup.

1973	
★★★★★	Blizzard GR models
★★★★	Blizzard 295, 340, 440
★★★	Blizzard 640, 797

1973

Grass racing was an important showcase for the snowmobile manufacturers in the early seventies. It allowed them the opportunity to show some of their new wares and their performance. Early in the summer of 1972, Bombardier introduced a series of grass racing Blizzard models. They were made in all class sizes. The engines from 440 down were new, twin-cylinder, rotary valve designs, while the 640 and 797 remained nearly unchanged from the 1972 models. The twins were all mounted in a new chassis that was based on what would be the winter chassis

The Blizzard name returned on the 1977 Blizzard oval racer. It was one of the three liquid-cooled models produced by Bombardier for the season. *Bombardier Corp.*

and the all-new T'NT F/A models. The Blizzard GRs had special rubber tracks with bogie wheel suspension. The chassis was stripped to its bare minimums with small fuel tanks and seats used, aluminum components were used extensively, and most of the engines were set up to run on methanol rather than gasoline since they were mod class machines. The 640 and 797 used a lightened version of the 1972 Blizzard chassis while the twins were installed on the new chassis with fiberglass belly pan and special hood. The Blizzard GRs are the rarest Blizzard models ever made.

The Blizzard models produced for the 1972-1973 winter season were spectacular looking sleds, particularly the twin-cylinder models which rode on the new chassis design. The new chassis was all-aluminum with a fiberglass hood that allowed the top end of the engine to protrude out of the hood. Again, the machine had no windshield. The thick seat had a very tall backrest, a design asked for by Bombardier's star racer, Yvon Duhamel. Yvon wanted to be able to lock himself into position on the sled and not have to crawl all over the machine to make it through the corners. The new front-engine chassis, carbide wear bars, and wider ski stances were producing sleds that made Yvon's request reasonable. A rider could lock in between the foot rests and the tall seat back and just let it fly.

The 640 and 797 were mounted on the 1972 chassis. The only changes made were the installation of new HD carburetors from Tillotson and the HP clutch. The HP clutch was a version of Polaris' clutch design, produced by Bombardier under license from Polaris.

1974	
Not ratable	Blizzard

1974

A 1974 model Blizzard was built as a Sno-Pro race sled only to be driven by Mike Trapp and Yvon Duhamel. The duo never hit the tracks as Bombardier withdrew from racing for the duration of the energy shortage. Trapp and Duhamel were kept under contract for

Ski-Doo's first production sleds with IFS were the 1978 Blizzard oval racers, built as Super Stock and Super Mod oval race sleds. Shown here is the Super Mod version. The Super Stock sleds had a black panel on the front of the hood. *Bombardier Corp.*

the season, working with snowmobile clubs, schools, and dealers, passing along personal racing tips and showing snowmobilers how to have "more fun with less gas." The 1974 Blizzard models were never seen in action.

The Blizzard name left the Ski-Doo line up for three years, surfacing again in 1977 as a limited-production, stock class race sled.

1977	
★★★★✦	Blizzard
★★★★★	Blizzard X models

1977

The 1977 Blizzard was built to meet all the stock class requirements of the day, including the sound level limits which were 78 dbA at 50 feet. There were actually two versions of the sled built. The two were identical with the exception that the "Michigan" version was equipped with a headlight and taillight to meet that state's particular stock class regulations. The chassis was an entirely new design with aluminum tunnel and welded steel front member. Aluminum extrusions were used to make the very short, snow and ice penetrating skis. An internal-drive, steel-cleated track was used and the engine was a wonderfully powerful 436.6cc, rotary valve,

1977 Blizzard 440 LC:	
Overall length	96in
Overall width	40in
Approx. weight	360lb
Ski stance	34.5 in
Fuel capacity	4.2 US gal
Track width	15in
Track length	111 7/8in
Bore	67.5mm
Stroke	61mm
Displacement	436.6cc
Carburetor	Two VM 44
Horsepower	98hp at 9250rpm

liquid-cooled twin. Heat exchangers for cooling the engine were mounted on each vertical side of the tunnel.

The engine was fitted with a new, 6-pole Bosch CDI and VM 44 Mikuni carburetors. A twin expansion chamber system flowed into a single "swirl chamber" silencer. The engine pumped out about 98hp at 9250rpm. Nikasil plating was used on the bores of the single exhaust port cylinders. A single "L" ring mounted at the top of the pistons.

The 1977 Blizzard 440 was the only stock class Blizzard produced for the season. There were, however, three Blizzard "X" models produced in very low numbers: 250, 340, 440. These sleds used the same basic chassis but were fitted with modified, liquid-cooled engines with unsilenced expansion chambers. The Blizzard "X" models ran in the modified classes only.

The clutch for the 1977 Blizzard models was a square shaft design utilizing two rollers pushing against replaceable ramps that were bolted to the governor bell. The design made the clutch more tunable by being able to change the profile of the ramp. The high rotational speed of the engine produced very high centrifugal forces in the clutch, however, and, in time, stretched the governor bell into an

The Blizzard name was first attached to a "consumer" sled on the 1978 Blizzard 6500 Plus. The machine was built on the R/V chassis and closely resembled the Cross Country racing sled of the previous season. *Bombardier Corp.*

oval shape. Later designs would use three ramps and rollers on the high performance engines to eliminate the problem.

1978	
★★★★	Blizzard 6500
★★★★⌐	Blizzard Super Stock
★★★★★	Blizzard Super Mod

The oval racing Blizzard models for 1979 had a new look as well as new technology. *Bombardier Corp.*

1978

There were seven Blizzard models for 1978 with two very different chassis designs and two very different applications in mind.

The Blizzard 6500 Plus was a consumer available, 339cc, liquid-cooled machine based on the T'NT R/V's chassis. About the only changes in the chassis over the R/V's was the use of a 4130 chrome-moly steel front cross member, heat exchangers mounted in the top of the tunnel and a 16 1/2in track. The Blizzard 6500 Plus was the top of the line for consumers in 1978 and with better than 65hp and the incredible handling of the R/V chassis, it was a great little scooter.

The 6500's engine was detuned from the racing version used the previous year in the R/V Cross Country. The engine had new crankcases with a different magneto set up and wider spacing between the two front cylinder studs to allow for the new, triple exhaust port. The cylinders had cast iron sleeves and the new ignition was mounted conventionally in the crankcase. The trigger coils for the new Bosch system mounted externally on the crankcase and timing could be adjusted while the engine was running. The ignition was a six pole design.

The six other Blizzard models for 1978 were all intended for serious racers. Bombardier's factory team had been racing with several independent front suspension (IFS) designs the preceding season but the 1978 Blizzard Super Stock and Super Mod sleds were the first production IFS sleds from Bombardier and, fittingly, they carried the Blizzard name. There was a 250, 340, and 440 in

both Super Stock and Super Mod trim.

Production of all-out racing sleds by many manufacturers had made a sham out of what were called the "Stock" classes. The United States Snowmobile Association (USSA) created what were called the Super Stock classes to accommodate these special sleds. The old "Stock" class rules were loosened a bit (sound level limits went out the window) and manufacturers were free to create the best production race sleds they could dream up.

There was very little difference between Ski-Doo's Super Stock and Super Mod version of the Blizzard models for 1978. The hood on the Super Stock version had a black panel in the middle of the hood while the Super Mod had an all-yellow hood. The mod engines were set up with dual ignition and two spark plugs per cylinder. Different pipes, a larger diameter sway bar, and a few minor differences defined the Super Mods from the Super Stocks.

The sleds shared the same basic chassis. The tunnels were aluminum and the front frame was an aircraft-like, tubular, steel frame. Twin, horizontal radius rods carried the swing arm which pivoted near the driver's foot on each side of the chassis. The tracks were internal-drive, steel-cleated types. All engines were liquid-cooled, rotary valve twins. A radiator in the nose of the machine was used rather than heat exchangers in the tunnel. All six race sleds were equipped with hydraulic brakes and a Bombardier, square shaft, three-ramp clutch.

1979 "Consumer" Blizzard Models			
	5500	7500	9500
Overall length	104in	107in	104in
Overall width	39in	41.8in	39in
Approx. weight	410lb	420lb	440lb
Ski stance	33.5in	34in	33.5in
Fuel cap. (US gal)	7.8	6.9	7.8
Track width	15in	16 1/2in	15in
Track length	114in	114in	114in
Bore	72mm	59.5mm	67.5mm
Stroke	61mm	61mm	61mm
Displacement	496.5cc	339cc	436.4cc
Carburetor	2 VM34	2 VM34	2 VM36
Horsepower	52hp	65hp	82hp

1979

Bombardier built six models with the Blizzard name for 1979. Three were race sleds and three were consumer sleds. There were 340 and 440 Super Stock, oval racing sleds (a 250cc version was built as a Moto-Ski.) and a Blizzard Cross Country race sled which was based on the Blizzard 7500. The big news for 1979 was the introduction of the Blizzard 5500 and the 9500.

A completely new, "monocoque" frame was designed for the new Blizzard models. The tunnel was aluminum and the front member-belly pan was a single welded piece made of High Strength, Low Alloy (HSLA) steel. The steel was a new alloy developed for the auto industry to make lighter body pan-

The oval racing Blizzard chassis was ultra light, utilizing an aluminum tunnel with a 4130 tubular steel front frame section. *Snow Goer Magazine*

els possible. The tunnel was unpainted and the front frame and belly pan was painted a metallic gray as were the skis and leaf springs. The hood was fiberglass and shaped like the cockpit area of a Formula I race car. The Blizzard 5500 and 9500 shared the same basic chassis.

A first, for a standard production sled, from Ski-Doo was the jackshaft-mounted driven pulley in the Blizzard 5500 and 9500. A mechanical, self-adjusting brake caliper was used. The suspension utilized large-diameter drive sprockets and rear idlers and a thin, all-new track. For the first time, Bombardier used a hexagonal drive axle with pressed-on plastic sprockets. The track could easily be pulled over by hand with the new design.

The 5500 received an all-new engine, the type 503 axial fan-cooled, piston-port twin. One of the interesting features on the new power plant was the "fan forced" muffler. A jacket surrounded the tuned exhaust system with an air space between it and the actual chamber of the exhaust system. A fitting in the cooling shroud of the engine allowed air to be taken from the engine and flowed through the jacket surrounding the muffler. Air exited the chamber from a tube that was concentric with the actual exhaust outlet. The design reduced under hood temperatures and lowered the sound level of the exhaust system.

A liquid-cooled, 436.6cc twin powered the 9500. The engine was a three-exhaust port, rotary valve, type 454 engine based on the race engines but equipped with cast iron sleeved cylinders. The 503 had a Bosch breaker point magneto while the 354 and 454 ran Bosch's 6-pole CDI.

The Blizzard 6500 of the previous season became the Blizzard 7500 in the 1979 line-up with few changes. This was the last year of production for what was known as the "R/V" chassis.

1980 ★★	Blizzard 5500, 7500, 9500

1980

No racing Blizzard models were built for the 1980 model year. The 5500 and 9500 returned with few changes and the 7500 was built on the new Blizzard chassis. The belly pans for 1980 remained gray but the skis were painted black by popular demand! The 5500 and 7500 had black hoods with yellow accents while the 9500 had a yellow hood with a black headlight area and accents. A front bumper/grab handle was added to all models. The frame was beefed up at the cross member and engine mounting area.

The Blizzard 9500 was fitted with a new

1979 introduced two completely new Blizzard models, the 9500 and the 5500. When you compare the styling on the Blizzard 9500, shown above, to the 1979 oval racing Blizzard, you can immediately see the influence of the race sled on the new consumer model. *Bombardier Corp.*

track. The lugs had a toothed pattern, there were staggered cleats at the outer edges of the track to control sideslip and fishtailing, and the entire surface of the track had a pebble finish.

1981

Eighty Formula 340 Ski-Doo Blizzard models were built for the 1980-1981 season. The race sleds were built as replicas of Jacques Villeneuve's Eagle River World Championship sled of the previous season.

The Blizzard 5500, 7500, and 9500 returned. The fuel tanks had plastic covers rather than the seat flowing up over them, and the 9500's hood was red with black accents. The 7500 was black with red accents while the 5500 was a more traditional yellow

Still known "inside" as a Blizzard model, eighty of these 1981 oval race sleds were built for qualified independent racers. The machine was a replica of the sled on which Jacques Villeneuve won the Eagle River World Championship. *Bombardier Corp.*

1981 Blizzard 5500MX Snowmobile By Ski-Doo
Front and Rear (Total) Suspension System

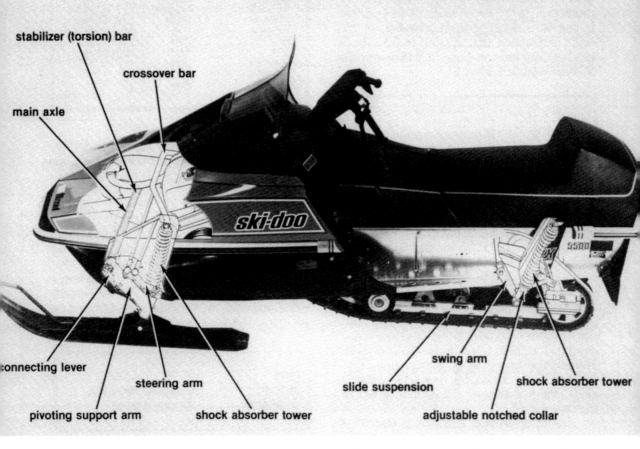

stabilizer (torsion) bar

crossover bar

main axle

connecting lever

steering arm

pivoting support arm

shock absorber tower

swing arm

slide suspension

shock absorber tower

adjustable notched collar

The 1981 Blizzard 5500MX was the first consumer-available IFS model from Ski-Doo. The rear suspension featured 10in of vertical travel, a figure snowmobile manufacturers are working up to again today. *Snow Goer Magazine*

and black. The six-pole Bosch CDI was replaced with a Nippon Denso, four-pole CDI system on the 7500 and 9500. The 503 engine stayed with the breaker point Bosch ignition.

An all-new model of the Blizzard was introduced late in the summer of 1980, the Blizzard 5500 MX. It was to be Ski-Doo's first consumer available IFS machine. The sled was a derivative of the Blizzard 5500, using its basic frame, engine, and driveline. In front was a trailing arm controlled by a hydraulic shock with concentric coil spring. Through the center of the pivot point of the trailing arm was the sway bar, attached to the trailing arms with a short levers. The track suspension was most impressive, offering 10in of travel! Many of the concepts in the long-travel rear suspension of the Blizzard MX are being rediscovered today as manufacturers search for more suspension travel. The Blizzard 5500 MX was intended to be a trail machine, capable of handling the enormous moguls that grow on the trails late on the weekend. It did just that. You could slam the MX through some terrible conditions and the sled was strong enough to take it and provide an astonishingly smooth ride. The big problem with the sled was that it was terrible in the snow. Even though intended for the trails, customers still wanted to be able to head off into the snow now and then and the MX just wouldn't allow it.

1982
★ ★ ★ ★   **Blizzard Formula 340**
★ ★   **Blizzard 5500 MX, 9500**

1983 Blizzard models

	MX	9700
Overall length	104in	104in
Overall width	39.5in	39.5in
Approx. weight	492lb	492lb
Ski stance	33.9in	33.5in
Fuel capacity	7.2 US gal	7.2 US gal
Track width	16 1/2in	16 1/2in
Track length	114in	114in
Bore	72mm	72mm
Stroke	61mm	64mm
Displacement	496.5cc	521.2cc
Carburetor	2 VM34	2 VM40
Horsepower	52hp	86hp

1982

A small number of Formula 340 Blizzard models were made for the 1981-1982 season with few changes from the previous year's racer. It was the last single-track, oval track race sled produced by Bombardier.

Two consumer Blizzard models remained in the line for 1982, the 5500 MX and the 9500. The 503 engine was fitted with Nippon Denso CDI and both engines were equipped with oil injection for the first time. The oil injection pump, on both engines, was fitted on the recoil starter, driven by a plastic shaft running through the drilled center of the starter shaft.

The track on both Blizzard models was widened to 16 1/2in, improving the MX's ability in snow and giving the 9500 more stability and traction. Both Blizzard models were classic combinations of Ski-Doo yellow and black for 1982.

The new model was called the Blizzard 9700. The oil injection pump for the new engine mounted on the rotary valve cover and was driven by the rotary valve shaft. A new cylinder head design included a two-way thermostat that allowed engine coolant to circulate through the engine and reservoir till the engine was up to operating temperature. The thermostat then gradually shifted flow through the heat exchangers. The design helped eliminate the chance of a cold seizure when operated by someone who just had to get on the throttle in a hurry!

1984
★ ★ ★   **Blizzard 5500 MX**
★ ★ ★ ⌐   **Blizzard 9700**

1984

Ski-Doo was celebrating its 25th anniversary in 1984. Many new models were introduced but the two Blizzard models remained basically unchanged from 1983. The Blizzard name disappeared from the Ski-Doo line with the 1984s. As is always the case, however, no one knows for sure when a Blizzard may strike again!

1983
★ ⌐   **Blizzard 5500 MX**
★ ★ ★   **Blizzard 9700**

1983

The Blizzard MX returned with virtually no changes. A new, type 534 engine replaced the type 454 in the top-of-the-line Blizzard.

The Blizzard 5500MX's front suspension featured trailing arms that allowed the skis to travel through an arc that moved the skis up and backward over a bump. *Snow Goer Magazine*

For 1983, the 9500 Blizzard with its type 454 engine was replaced by the 9700 Blizzard and its type 534 engine. *Snow Goer Magazine*

The Twin-Track Racer

Rejean Beauregard was the designer behind the tube frame Blizzard oval track racing sleds, and was the key designer for Ski-Doo's twin-track race sled project. Working with Beauregard was Gaeton Duval, who helped develop the sled and took over the entire twin-track program when Beauregard left the company. Certainly a lot of inspiration and initial set-up of the machine was provided by Jacques Villeneuve, who was campaigning a Formula Atlantic race car as well as racing for Ski-Doo. Villeneuve's involvement with very specialized race cars had to be a big advantage for Beauregard and Duval.

Ski-Doo's first twin-track race sled was built for the winter of 1980-1981. The machine, like most oval race sleds, was designed to turn to the left more efficiently than to the right, and was totally asymmetric. Race rules required 15in of track width, so the twin-tracker was fitted with two 7 1/2in-wide, steel-cleated tracks. The driver was positioned over the left-side track and the engine was positioned in front of the left tunnel as well. Overall width at the outside edges of the skis was 45in as was the width of the tunnel at the rear of the machine.

The ski suspension system was a side swing arm design with four transverse radius rods, similar to what was being used on the single-track race sleds. Two small torque reaction systems handled the rear suspension of the tracks.

The chaincase fed torque to the drive axles at the center of the chassis, between the tracks. The right-side drive axle was coupled directly to a splined collar turned by the drive sprocket. Torque to the left side drive axle was fed through a multi-plate friction clutch borrowed from Bombardier's Can-Am motorcycle. The release lever for the clutch connected with a cable to the steering shaft. As soon as the handlebars were turned to the left, the clutch would disconnect the torque fed to the left track and all torque went to the right track, literally forcing the machine around the corner. When you felt like you might not make it

through a corner on a twin-track, it was usually a matter of giving it more throttle, not less, to squeak the machine through the turn!

The first twin-tracker was fitted with an air foil or wing on the front of the hood to provide additional down pressure on the skis when at speed. It didn't take too many spills before the wing was removed from the sled for good. Later body designs incorporated a shape that provided the aerodynamic down pressure to the skis.

Race rules limited engine displacement to 340cc in the Formula I class in which the twin-track was competing. The type 354 Rotax so dominated the class that it became the only engine used by all racers in the Formula I class. By the early nineties, the rotary valve, liquid-cooled twin was pumping out more than 100hp from its 339.2cc while turning between 10,800 and 11,200rpm. The 354 race engine was the highest specific output engine ever used in a snowmobile, producing 295hp per liter of displacement while running on gasoline!

The first appearance of the RAVE valve on a snowmobile engine was on a twin-track race sled. In 1985, Michel Gingras picked up the Eagle River World Championship the very first time the RAVE-equipped 354 was run in competition. The type 354 engine has been refined every year and has more World Championships to its credit than any other engine ever built.

The first major change in suspension was made available to racers on the 1985 twin-track. An "A" arm front suspension designed by Dave Karpik, who was working with Gaeton Duval and Brad Hulings, was developed, along with a single aluminum extrusion that became the unique slide rail design of the twin-tracker.

Ski-Doo's twin-track oval race sled so dominated its class that the last time a single-track machine won a World Championship was in 1984. While a few single-track designs have tried to compete against the twin-tracker since 1984, the overwhelming cornering ability of the twin-track racer is simply too much to give up.

Former Eagle River World Champion Gary Vessair on his 1983 Ski-Doo twin-track, oval race sled. *Bombardier Corp.*

Above and right: The Blizzard name left the Ski-Doo line-up with the 1984 Blizzard 9700 and Blizzard 5500MX. *Snow Goer Magazine*

Chapter 8

The Elan

1971-1995
What became the Élan grew out of a study to create a child's snowmobile, a machine similar to Arctic Cat's Kitty Cat. What was discovered in the course of the project was that a small machine with a full sized 15x114in track and a single-cylinder engine could be built at the same cost as a tiny machine for children. A machine was put together following the classic principles of J. Armand's first Ski-Doo. An all-steel chassis with a fiberglass hood mounted a 247cc, single-cylinder engine on top of the tunnel. The track was Ski-Doo's classic 15x114in rubber track with steel reinforcing rods. The suspension was a bogie wheel design but each of the three sets of bogies mounted three rather than four wheels. The skis were only 30 1/2in long and had no grab handle at their tips. A pivoting arm type brake was used, pressing on the fixed half of the chaincase-mounted driven pulley. It may seem strange that an electric start version of the Élan was offered but even with a decompressor valve in the cylinder, the 247 single could be a handful for a small person to pull over. If the machine was to be the perfect beginner's and children's machine, it had to be easy to start. With a suggested retail price of $595, the new little machine would invite many to the world of snowmobiling. The new creation was named Élan, a French word meaning, enthusiasm, vigor, impetuosity. The name was perfect for the sprightly little machine!

The Élan continues to this day as an icon of J. Armand's original concepts. The little machine has had many changes through the years, most of them subtle. Each time the changes strayed too far from the original concept, the strength of its origin has pulled it back. I shall attempt to list the major changes to the Élan and in what years those changes occurred.

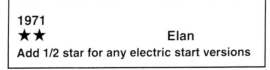

1971	
★★	Elan
Add 1/2 star for any electric start versions	

1971
Right off the bat the go-fast bunch was looking at the Élan's light weight as a key to speed. Along with the original version, a 250 Blizzard version of the Élan was built as a

Original Élan (1971)	
Overall length	88 1/2in
Overall width	29.1in
Approx. weight	246lb/E 282lb
Ski stance	23in
Fuel capacity	4.4 US gal
Track width	15in
Track length	114in
Suspension	Bogie wheel
Bore	69mm
Stroke	66mm
Displacement	247cc
Carburetor	Tillotson HR
Horsepower	12hp

A study of a little machine for children resulted in the Elan, featuring a full-size, 15X114in track as a 1971 model. Suggested retail for the new little machine was $595.00. *J-A Bombardier Museum*

1971 model. While the 250 Blizzard was intended for use in Europe, a small number were sprinkled around North America.

1972	
★✈	Elan
★★★	Elan 292 SS

1972

The first year of the Élan showed the need to strengthen the frame with angle iron extensions in the engine support area that run to the front of the frame. The ski blade remained the same but a handle/reinforcement was added to its tip. The two forward sets of bogie wheels had a fourth wheel added while the rear set remained unchanged with three wheels. The hood material was polycarbonate for 1972 and an SS 292 version of the Élan was built. The 292 was the same engine used in the T'NT, producing 22hp. Most SS 292 Élans were sold in the Eastern United States and Canada. The weight of the Élan increased by about 6lb in 1972.

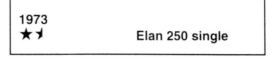

1973	
★✈	Elan 250 single

1973

Four Élan models were built for 1973. The 247 and its electric start version were joined by two new twin-cylinder engines also displacing 247cc. The type 248 engine was the same as the type 249 engine used in the SS model but was in a milder state of tune. The 249 powered the Élan SS and had dual HR carburetors and a tuned exhaust system while the milder 248 engine had a single HR carb and standard muffler. The 248 produced 16hp while the 249 made 22hp.

The two twin-cylinder models were equipped with a ski leg that bent out at 90 degrees at its bottom for increased ski stance and improved stability. Ski stance stretched out to 25.5in with the new ski legs. The SS model had a mechanical disk caliper brake while the other models used the standard pivoting arm brake.

All Élans received a high/low beam headlight, voltage regulator, padded handlebar, brake light, and emergency shut-off switch on the handlebar. Ball joints were used for the first time on the tie rod ends on the Élan in 1973, as was the round-shaft roller clutch.

1974	
★✦	Elan single
★★	Elan T and DL
★★★	Elan SS

1974

A black polycarbonate hood was used on the Élan SS and Deluxe models for 1974. The SS was powered by a 293cc twin, a bored and stroked version of the 250 twin, while the Deluxe and 250 T was powered by the type 248 engine. The 293cc engine mounted a single HR carburetor and produced 24hp. The 250 twin- and single-cylinder engines remained relatively unchanged with exception of bearing and seal changes on the crankshaft of the twin.

A new driven pulley with a brake drum rolled onto its flange was used to allow use of the drum type brake. The 294 SS was set up with a square-shaft, two-roller clutch while the rest of the line ran the round-shaft roller clutch. The entire Élan line was fitted with forged, offset ski legs pushing the stance out to 25.5in. Hydraulic shock absorbers were standard on the skis of the SS and Deluxe models in 1974. An all-steel slide suspension was standard equipment on the 294 SS, a first for the Élan. At 330lb, the 1974 Élan SS was the heaviest Élan ever built.

1975	
★✦	Elan single
★★	Elan twin

1975

An interesting styling concept was tried by Bombardier with the Élans for 1975. The 300 SS (powered by the 293cc engine) and the Deluxe had black hoods while the single-

Elan was given two versions of a twin-cylinder, 247.3cc engine for 1973. The Elan SS featured a tuned exhaust system and twin HR carburetors while the Elan 250T was fitted with a standard muffler and single HR carburetor. *J-A Bombardier Museum*

Slide suspension was a feature added to the Elan SS in 1974. *Bombardier Corp.*

cylinder model had a white hood. A set of decals was available that had various color combinations in it and caricatures of a fox and a group of penguins. The customer had the opportunity to select the styling he or she wanted on the Élan. The combinations were intended for use on the white hoods only but many of the combinations ended up on the SS and Deluxe models as well.

There was no "E" model of the 247 Élan for 1975. Instead, all the single-cylinder engines were equipped with electric starters. A kit with battery, hold-down, and wiring was sold as an accessory for those who wanted electric start. Evidently inventories of the 247 engines with starter and ring gear were high and it was decided to use them on all the single-cylinder Élans built that year.

Slide suspension was again standard on the 300 SS. All other models were set up with three sets of four bogie wheels. The fuel tank was made slightly smaller (4.2 US gal) to allow for growth of the polyethylene tank without its binding in the frame.

1976-1979	
★↗	**Elan single**
★★	**Elan twin**

1976

An electric and manual start version of the 247 single was offered for 1976 along with the type 248 twin. Slide suspension disappeared from the Élans. The ski was new for 1976 with an additional reinforcement welded on the top side near the curve of the ski. The 247 and 247 E were fitted with a white hood while the Deluxe retained its black hood.

1977

The 247 Élan was offered in a manual start version only. Electric start was never offered on the Élan again. There were no significant changes to the Élan Deluxe.

1978

An aluminum-rail, torque-reaction suspension was standard equipment on the Élan Deluxe. No other significant changes were made to the two Élan models.

1979

The Élan's chassis had always been painted black. For 1979, the chassis and skis were painted metallic gray like the rest of the Ski-Doo line. Both Élan models used the black polycarbonate hood. The single-cylinder 247 and the twin-cylinder 248 were both available. The slide rail suspension was replaced with a bogie suspension on the Deluxe model. Slides were never available again on the Élan. This was also the final year for the twin-cylinder, type 248 engine.

1980-1995

For 1980 the type 247 engine received a larger bore, 69.5mm, increasing the displacement from 247cc to 250.4cc. The engine was also set up with a VM28 Mikuni carburetor and remote fuel pump. The 1980 Élan was the prototype for the next fifteen years.

In the years following 1980, there were minor calibration changes and improvements made. The Élan was never equipped with CDI or oil injection. Hood shapes and colors changed but technically, the Élan remained virtually unchanged.

1995 Élan	
Overall length	88.5in
Overall width	30.5in
Approx. weight	284lb
Ski Stance	25.5in
Fuel capacity	3.6 US gal
Track width	15in
Track length	114in
Suspension	Bogie wheel
Bore	69.5mm
Stroke	66mm
Displacement	250.4cc
Carburetor	Mikuni VM28
Horsepower	12hp

As a spruced-up, mid-nineties kind of guy, the venerable Elan continues its dependable ways for 1995 based on the lessons it learned from its 1980 cousin. *Snow Goer Magazine*

The 1980 Elan was the prototype for the next fifteen years with its 15x114in track, bogie suspension, 250.4cc single-cylinder engine with Mikuni carburetor, and incredible dependability. *J-A Bombardier Museum*

Chapter 9

The Elite

★ ★ ★ ★	1973 Elite

1973

Creative concepts were rampant at Bombardier in the early seventies. Designs of all natures were studied and operating prototypes of some concepts were actually built. Perhaps the most interesting was the Mirage II. Powered by a 1600cc, four-cylinder Ford industrial engine, the twin-tracked machine could seat four in totally enclosed comfort. Two 20-in-wide deep-profile tracks provided floatation. The machine was brought to distributor meetings where demonstration rides were given and the concept discussed.

A year before the Mirage II was getting attention, about October of 1972, the first prototype of the Elite was being tested and its aesthetic design finalized. When looking at the two machines, one can see several design similarities, though the Elite was a much smaller machine.

The original Elite was powered by a type 434, 436.4cc, electric start Rotax making 28hp. The fan-cooled engine's cooling air was not well ducted in and out of the rear engine compartment and vapor lock was a common occurrence with the original design, even though Ski-Doo's unique, snow-cooled muffler was used on the Elite in an effort to lower

1973 Elite:	
Overall length	103in
Overall width	44in
Approx. weight	682lb
Ski stance	34.8in
Fuel capacity	6.4 US gal
Track width	2x15in
Track length	2x114in
Bore	67.5mm
Stroke	61mm
Displacement	436.4cc
Carburetor	Tillotson HD
Horsepower	28hp

engine compartment temperatures. A single Tillotson HD carburetor fed the engine.

The forward/reverse gearbox was the same one used on the Alpine and Valmont models that year. Because of the Elite's weight—682lb—a larger diameter brake disk and mechanical caliper were used on the gearbox.

Two 15x114in tracks mounted on a bogie wheel suspension. The two bucket seats mounted forward on the track tunnels and the riders' feet rested in the belly pan area of the machine, a very comfortable position. The passenger's side was equipped with a seat belt and a grab handle on the dash. The instrument panel included a speedometer, tachometer, and electric fuel gauge. The instrument pod was similar to the one used on the Nordic model that year.

The frame and belly pan was made of steel and the upper body was fiberglass. A small roll bar mounted on the body behind

The Mirage II was a concept machine that grew out of the original Elite designs. Demonstration rides given at distributor meetings in 1973 gener-ated lots of discussion and dreams for the future. *Bombardier Inc.*

the riders. Dual headlights and taillights gave the vehicle the look of an automobile.

shaft clutch. Minor changes were made throughout the machine.

★★★★	1974 Elite

★★★★	1975 Elite

1974

The Elite received a larger, 8.1 US gal, fuel tank and the engine compartment was enlarged by raising the height of the rear deck. A new engine shroud and outlet duct helped control the vapor lock problem encountered the year before. The carburetor was recalibrated and the engine was fitted with a square

1975

Like the two previous years, the 1975 Elite had a white body and a black frame. There was virtually no change in the Elite for the year and it was to be the last of the original concept Elite models. Another three seasons passed before the Elite returned to the Ski-Doo line-up.

★ ★ ★ ★ ◢   **1978 Elite**

1978

An all-new Elite was unveiled for 1978 and it was finished like a classic Ski-Doo with a black frame and yellow body. Wood-grained decals highlighted the vertical sides of the body. A liquid-cooled, type 444, rotary valve engine with a single Mikuni VM 34 carburetor powered the Elite. Electric handlebar heaters improved driver comfort and a "V" belt-driven, 35amp automotive alternator provided all the power that was needed for stereo radios or any other accessory one wanted to add. The dashboard was specifically designed to accept a radio and other add-ons.

The engine compartment was fitted with an automotive type radiator and a fan mounted on the magneto end of the crankshaft. Large louvers on the right side

1978 Elite	
Overall length	107in
Overall width	44.5in
Approx. weight	790lb
Ski stance	34.5in
Fuel capacity	8.3 US gal
Track width	2-15in
Track length	2-120in
Bore	69.5mm
Stroke	57.5mm
Displacement	436cc
Carburetor	Mikuni VM 34
Horsepower	48hp

of the body allowed air in. The fan moved the air over the radiator and out the left side of the engine compartment. The crankshaft-mounted fan precluded the use of a recoil starter so the governor bell of the clutch was equipped with a flange to allow the engine to be started with a rope if the battery wasn't up to snuff. A twin-chamber muffler exhausted into a long tail pipe that ran to the right rear corner of the machine.

The 6in-longer tracks rode on twin torque reaction slide suspension assemblies, improving the ride of the Elite considerably over the original models. A practical storage compart-

ment was added to the front of the body ahead of the riders' legs. Instrumentation included speedometer, tachometer, electric fuel gauge, and engine coolant temperature. Of course, the Elite retained its forward/reverse transmission and electric starter.

★ ★ ★ ★ ◢   **1979 Elite**

1979

The early type 444 Rotax engine used a cylinder and head that had been designed for use in the Can-Am motorcycle. The situation was the same as that experienced with the first liquid-cooled Everest model. The dome of the cylinder head did not cool well in the snowmobile application. For 1979, a new cylinder head with full water jackets was used on the Elite. Other changes were minor.

★ ★ ★ ★ ◢   **1980 Elite**

1980

An ignition damping box was added between the two ignition coils. The device contained a diode in series with a resistor and was used to stop errant signals from the breaker points that could fire the coils at inappropriate times, leading to engine overheating.

★ ★ ★ ★ ★   **1981 Elite**

1981

An all-black paint job with gold pin-striping and gold upholstery on the bucket seats made the Elite an elegant-looking machine but the Elite had a new heart, too. The new, type 464 engine was equipped with Nippon Denso electronic ignition and oil injection. With 57hp, the engine added new zip as well as convenience to the Elite.

The original 1973 Elite was powered by a 440cc, fan-cooled engine and featured the side-by-side seating that made the Elite unique and a favorite with its fans. *Bombardier Inc.*

The 464 Rotax was a completely new engine, bearing little resemblance to the 444. While the 444 utilized a single, Siamese cylinder casting, the 464 had separate cylinders. The rotary valve shaft of the 464 was also used to drive the valve cover-mounted oil injection pump. Basic specifications for the new engine looked like this:

Bore	69.5mm
Stroke	61mm
Displacement	462.8cc
Carburetor	1 VM 34 Mikuni
Ignition	Nippon Denso CDI
Horsepower	57hp

Modifications were made to the Elite to accept the new engine but few other changes were made to the basic machine.

★★★★★   1982 Elite

1982

A pair of "ox horn" handlebars and a new aluminum governor cup were about all that changed on the Elite for 1982. The bucket seat Ski-Doo left the line-up following the 1981-1982 season. The Elite was an intriguing machine, one many have never seen on the trails. There is a strong following of faithful Elite owners who have rebuilt their machines many times as they consider the possibility of its return. Today's trail systems combined with a renewed interest in two-up touring seem to beckon for its return.

In 1978, the Elite was totally new with slide rail suspension, a 444cc liquid-cooled engine and a new chassis and hood design. *Bombardier Corp.*

The final Elite was built as a 1982 model. Powered by the oil-injected, type 464, liquid-cooled engine, the machine still has a devoted following that longs for a new generation Elite. *Bombardier Corp.*

Everest

1977 Everest models			
	340/E	440/E	444 L/C
Overall length	105.8in	105.8in	105.8in
Overall width	35.5in	36.3in	36.3in
Approx. weight	380/400lb	411/435lb	475lb
Ski stance	28in	28in	28in
Fuel capacity	7.2 US gal	7.2 US gal	7.2 US gal
Track width	16 1/2in	16 1/2in	16 1/2
Track length	124in	124in	124in
Bore	59.5mm	67.5mm	69.5mm
Stroke	61mm	61mm	57.5mm
Displacement	339cc	436cc	436cc
Carburetor	Tillotson HD	Mikuni VM 34	VM 34
Horsepower	32hp	42hp	50hp

1977

Everest was the name given to the long-track T'NT 440 in 1974. The model continued as a member of the T'NT family until 1977 when it separated from the T'NT line to become the lux-

ury leader for Ski-Doo. Except for a very small build of 444 L/C Everest models built late in the 1975-1976 season, the Everest had always been a 440 fan-cooled machine. As its own line for 1977, there were five Everest models. A 340, using the type 343 twin-cylinder engine, was offered in manual and electric start. The chassis was essentially the same as the 440's but the hood was a yellow version of the 1976 T'NT hood. The 340 was equipped with a Tillotson HD carburetor. A separate Mikuni fuel pump supplied the carb but the carburetor was still prone to vapor lock when temperatures were high. Conversion to a Mikuni, float type carburetor totally eliminated the condition.

Everest separated from the T'NT line for 1977. The smallest model was the 340 which still carried the "T'NT look" hood design. *Bombardier Corp.*

The Everest 440 was available in manual or electric start. Its polycarbonate hood was black as was the belly pan. The 444 L/C was fitted with a yellow version of the same hood and the belly pan was painted gray. Electric start, handlebar heaters, rearview mirror, and plaid seat cover were standard on the L/C. Both the 444 and 440 were equipped with Mikuni carburetors.

1978

For 1978, the 340 was given the latest Everest hood and a VM 30 Mikuni carburetor. All the Everest models had a yellow hood in 1978. A plaid seat cover was used on the 440 as well as the 444 L/C. The bumper on the 440 and 340 was painted black along with the belly pans while the 444 L/C had a chrome-plated bumper and gray belly pan. Little else changed on the Everest models for 1978.

1979

The polycarbonate hood was unchanged for 1979 but an extension was added behind the headlight assembly. The extension moved the headlight forward and away from a horizontal ledge that could trap snow in front of the headlight. All the Everest models had gray belly pans and skis. A yellow hood was used on the 444 L/C while the 340 and 440 had a black hood. The plaid seat cover disappeared. Very few changes were made mechanically to the Everest models.

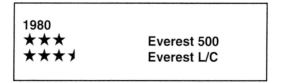

1980

The Everest received a lengthened version of the Blizzard's monocoque frame and a new fiberglass hood. The aluminum tunnel was left unpainted, the belly pans were painted gray and the hoods on both models were black. Two new engines powered the Everest models, leaving the track as about the only thing on the 1980 Everest models that wasn't new. The new chassis was equipped with a jackshaft-mounted driven pulley and the chaincase was on the right side of the frame. A brake disk mounted on the jackshaft and a self-adjusting, mechanical caliper mounted on the chaincase.

1980 Everest models:		
	500/E	L/C
Overall length	109in	109in
Overall width	39in	39in
Approx. weight	449/475lb	496lb
Ski stance	33.5in	33.5in
Fuel capacity	7.8 US gal	7.8 US gal
Track width	16 1/2in	16 1/2in
Track length	124in	124in
Bore	72mm	69.5mm
Stroke	61mm	61mm
Displacement	496.7cc	462.8cc
Carburetor	VM 36	VM 34
Horsepower	48hp	57hp

The Everest 500, offered with manual or electric start, was powered by a single-carb version of the 503 engine. The tuned muffler featured Ski-Doo's fan-forced design where cooling air from the engine was piped to a jacket enclosing the muffler. The air flow around the muffler lowered the temperatures under the hood and lowered the sound level at the outlet of the muffler.

The type 464 engine replacing the 444 was entirely new and offered oil injection for the first time on an Everest model. The oil injection pump mounted on the rotary valve cover and was driven by the rotary valve shaft. Electric start was standard on the 464 engine. The 503 and 464 were both equipped with a Bosch breaker point magneto.

1981

Black was the color for the belly pans in 1981 with a gray hood with black accents on the L/C and a black hood with gray accents on the 500. A new, wrap-around aluminum bumper was used on both models. The 464, liquid-cooled engine was equipped with Nippon Denso CDI and the 503 engine received oil injection. The injection pump for the 503 mounted on the recoil starter, driven by a plastic shaft connecting through the recoil starter shaft to the crankshaft.

Above and below: The 1977 fan-cooled 440 Everest featured a black hood and belly pan while the 444 LC Everest featured a gray belly pan and yellow hood. *Bombardier Corp.*

1982

The 503 engine was fitted with Nippon Denso electronic ignition. A new seat and fuel tank configuration were used. At 7.2 US gallons, the new tank was slightly smaller than the previous tank. Rather than the seat running up over the tank, the tank now had a separate, plastic cover. Like the previous tank, the new design was equipped with a sight gauge on the left side.

1983

There were no changes in the Everest for its final year.

Above: The final year for the Everest series was 1983. Offered with the type 503, fan-cooled engine and the 464, liquid-cooled engine, both still featured the bi-level seat. Shown here is the 1983 Everest L/C model. *Snow Goer Magazine*

Next page: For 1980, the Everest was put on a stretched version of the Blizzard chassis and offered with a type 503 fan-cooled engine or an electric start, type 464, liquid-cooled engine with electric start. *Snow Goer Magazine*

Chapter 11

The Citation

★★★⭐	1978 Citation
Add 1/2 star for any electric start versions	

1978 Citation	
Overall length	90in
Overall width	33in
Approx. weight	329lb
Ski stance	29.3in
Fuel capacity	5.5 US gal
Track width	15in
Track length	114in
Bore	57mm
Stroke	57.5mm
Displacement	293.3cc
Carburetor	Mikuni VM 30
Horsepower	24hp

1978

The first Citation used a shortened version of the Olympique chassis. Skis similar to the Élan's also helped keep the overall length of the Citation down. Offset ski legs gave the Citation a 3in-wider ski stance than the Olympique had. The little machine had all the features of the big sleds like a forward-mounted engine, aluminum chaincase, self-adjusting disk brake, torque-reaction slide suspension, shocks on the skis, smooth twin-cylinder engine, and instant torque drive pulley.

You'll recall from the Olympique chapter that the 1978 , were using a system called "tornado cooling." A separate compartment under the hood contained the muffler and cooling air from the engine was ducted into the compartment to take away the heat liberated by the muffler. The system worked well but it took up space that wasn't going to be available on the little Citation. A clever engineer in Valcourt decided to shrink the compartment down to simply a jacket around the muffler and bleed only a portion of the air moving through the engine's cooling shrouds to the jacket. A few tests confirmed the value of the concept and the fan-forced muffler was born!

The all-new Citation 4500 for 1980 was one of Ski-Doo's first models to be equipped with oil injection. *Snow Goer Magazine*

The Citation had a very low, fiberglass hood that was black with yellow side decals. The steel chassis was painted sliver to make it look lighter. A type 294 twin fitted with a Mikuni VM 30 carburetor powered the Citation:

1979	
★★★↙	**Citation**

1979

The Citation remained virtually unchanged for the 1979 model year.

1980	
★★★	**Citation (all models)**

1980

The 1980 Citation series replaced the Olympique series and the original Citation. Its completely new chassis was a monocoque design. The tunnel was aluminum and the front section, including the belly pan, which wrapped up above the height of the seat, was welded steel. Two different length tunnels were used. A short tunnel with a 106in long track was used for the single-cylinder 3500 model and the spirited SS model. The 4500 used a longer tunnel with 114in-long track. Other than the length of the rails, the torque-reaction slide suspension under the machines was identical.

A shortened Olympique chassis was used to build the 1978 and 1979 Citation 300. Limited space under the small hood inspired the "fan forced" muffler. *Bombardier Corp.*

1980 Citation models			
	3500	**4500/E**	**SS**
Overall length	98in	103.5in	98in
Overall width	36.5in	36.5in	36.5in
Approx. weight	327lb	353/380lb	352lb
Ski stance	32.3in	32.3in	32.3in
Fuel capacity	7.8 US gal	7.8 US gal	7.8 US gal
Track width	15in	15in	15in
Track length	106in	114in	106in
Bore	72mm	62mm	62mm
Stroke	66mm	61mm	61mm
Displacement	268.6cc	368.2cc	368.2cc
Carburetor	VM 34	VM 34	2 VM 30
Horsepower	28hp	35hp	40hp

The new Citation models were equipped with a cast-aluminum, jackshaft-mounted driven pulley. To allow the engine to be centered in the chassis, the driven pulley mounted over the tunnel on the shaft rather than at the end of the shaft. A support bearing on the left end of the jack-

Previous page: Longer duration porting and dual VM-30 carbs made the 1980 Citation SS a great performer (top). The 1980 Citation 3500 introduced a new single-cylinder engine to the Ski-Doo line-up, the type 277 (bottom). *Snow Goer Magazine*

shaft mounted in a hinged support that could be opened with a quick-release latch. On the chaincase end of the shaft, a bearing with a floating inner race secured the shaft to the case. With the left side bearing released from its support, the shaft could be lifted far enough to change the drive belt. A square shaft clutch was used on the SS while the 3500 and 4500 were fitted with round shaft roller clutches.

A brake disk mounted on the outer cam of the driven pulley. The brake caliper was a manually adjusted scissors type affair. Adjustment was made by rotating a length adjustment in the brake cable housing.

The hood on the new Citation models was more like a lid than a hood. Because the sides of the chassis came up so high on the sides, the hood didn't have to have much depth. Polycarbonate was used as the hood material. Black was the color for the 3500 and 4500, while the SS version was yellow. Seats on the new Citation models were very thick and very soft, adding greatly to the comfort of the ride.

Two completely new engines were introduced on the Citation and a high-performance version of the twin was used on the Citation SS. The 3500 was powered by a type 277, single-cylinder, fan-cooled engine while the 4500 and SS models used the new type 377, twin-cylinder engine. The SS version of the 377 engine had longer duration ports than the 4500's and dual carburetors. All the engines were sparked by Bosch breaker point magnetos. Oil injection was standard on the 4500, which was offered in manual and electric start versions. Also new on the Citation engines, and most of the Ski-Doo line for 1980, was the first major design change of the recoil starter. The metal pawls that engaged against a steel hub were replaced with plastic components that engaged positively with

each other. All engines were mounted with a new, three-point mounting system which attached to the engine at the ends of the crankcase rather than the bottom.

1981

Wrap-around, aluminum front bumpers were added to the SS and 4500 and the 3500 was fitted with a bumper that offered some protection at the corners of the chassis. Oil injection was added to the 3500 and the SS was fitted with dual 34mm carburetors. Black hoods were used on the SS and 4500

The Nordik name returned to Ski-Doo, spelled with a "k" this time, as a late-season-introduction 1981 model on a stretched-out Citation chassis with a 15x124in track. *J-A Bombardier Museum*

while the 3500 got the yellow hood for 1981.

The already popular Citation series spun off a new version for 1981, the Nordik. Its introduction was made mid season and did not officially join the line till 1982. The Nordik was basically a Citation 4500 with a 124in long track, ski legs with no offset, giving the Nordik a ski stance of 30in, a high windshield and no oil injection.

1982

Oil injection was added to the SS and it was put on the longer, 4500 chassis with 114in track. All engines were fitted with Nippon Denso electronic ignition and some 277s were equipped with a decompressor valve for easier starting. The series received few other changes for 1982.

Two Citation permutations officially joined the ranks in 1982, the Nordik and the Scandic. Both were intended as utility sleds with deep snow capability. They were powered by the 377 engine as used in the 4500 but had no oil injection system. The Nordik used a 15x124in track while the Scandic was fitted with a 15x139in track. The Scandic had a cargo rack at the rear of its extended tunnel. Unlike the Citation models, the Nordik used a ski leg with no offset, giving it a ski stance of 30in. The Scandic used the standard ski leg for a stance of 32.3in. A very high windshield with side "wings" was used on the Scandic. Both sleds were fitted with an orange polycarbonate hood and a heavy duty towing hitch.

1983

The SS model had its aluminum tunnel painted black for 1983 and new aluminum bumpers and bold graphics made it the best looking Citation yet. Little else changed on the bullet proof Citation series.

A 277, single-cylinder model of the long track Skandic was added to the Nordik/Scandic models. The new 277, like the other Nordiks and Scandiks, had no oil injection. Other changes were minor for 1983.

1984

The Citation series was reduced to the single-cylinder 3500. Both the 4500 and the SS models were dropped. No significant changes were made in the 3500.

The Citation LS was introduced in 1985 and was powered by the new, axial fan-cooled, single-cylinder, type 253 engine. Shown here is a 1988 Citation LS with its red hood with white stripe to match the Formula Plus of the year. *Snow Goer Magazine*

The Nordik and Scandic 277 were also dropped for 1984. The Scandic with its 377 engine was offered with or without reverse. The standard version still utilized the jackshaft arrangement to mount the driven pulley and the chaincase was on the right side of the chassis. The "R" model utilized an all-new, planetary type gearbox/chaincase. The assembly mounted on the left side of the chassis.

While the standard model was equipped with a driven pulley mounted brake disk and scissors-type caliper, the "R" model mounted a brake on the right end of the drive axle and used a more conventional mechanical caliper. The "R" was equipped with a parking brake activated by a separate handle and brake cable on the front of the right side handlebar.

Citation LS, Tundra, and Tundra LT

1985

The Scandic and Scandic R models remained in the line essentially unchanged for the 1985 and 1986 model years. Only the Scandic R was produced on the old Citation chassis design for 1987 and it was joined by a new Scandic 503 on a stretched Safari chassis.

An all-new Citation was unveiled as a 1985 model, the Citation LS. It was said by some that "LS" stood for Little Snowmobile and others said Light Snowmobile. Whichever was true, they were both accurate. The new little machine weighed under 300lb and was only 95.3in long.

The new Citation had an all-steel frame with a polyethylene belly pan and a Reaction In-jection Molded (RIM) urethane hood. The new hood material was tough and flexible. The forward-mounted, single-cylinder engine was a new design from Bombardier-Rotax.

There are many amazing stories of how native Canadians improvised ways to keep their Ski-Doos running when faced with problems. When out on a hunt in desolate territory, keeping the machine running was often a matter of life or death. Torn tracks were stitched together with leather straps, pistons with holes through the domes were repaired with carriage bolts, tree limbs were lashed between skis as tie rods but the most interesting story I ever heard was of a fellow who's 377 engine broke a PTO side connecting rod.

As the story goes, the engine was locked up solid with the rod hanging out through the badly broken crankcase. In his shop, the owner pulled the engine apart, sawed off the crankcase between the cylinders and, using his vise, pressed the PTO end of the crankshaft onto the right half of the MAG side crank half. He

An even longer version of the Citation chassis was introduced as the Skandic in 1982. The ex-tended chassis, housing a 15x139in track, was fitted with a cargo rack. *Snow Goer Magazine*

mounted the carburetor on the MAG side cylinder, cut down the fan shrouds and made himself a single-cylinder version of the axial fan-cooled engine!

The story made its way to Valcourt and eventually several of the engineers saw the amazing little engine for themselves. It is claimed that the cleverly salvaged engine prompted the design of the type 253 engine which was used to power the new Citation LS.

The new engine was designed to be lightweight, compact, and inexpensive to produce. It utilized a blind bore cylinder and head that was attached to the crankcase with four studs that ran all the way through the crankcase. The engine was equipped with Nippon Denso electronic ignition and oil injection. Of course, it utilized a belt-driven axial cooling fan rather than a large diameter flywheel-mounted fan used on all previous single-cylinder engine designs. An electric start version of the engine was also available.

A cast aluminum chaincase with stamped steel cover was used. The driven pulley mounted on the chaincase and carried a disk for the brake. The engine was equipped with a round-shaft roller clutch.

The track was the shortest ever used on a Ski-Doo at 102.4in. It was an internal-drive design and had a new, chevron traction pattern. The slide suspension was a stamped steel design with a shock absorber on the rear arm.

Two stretched versions of the Citation LS were produced as 1985 models, the Tundra with a 124in long track and the Tundra LT with a 139in long track. These two machines utilized

1985 Citation LS, Tundra and Tundra LT			
	Citation LS/E	Tundra	Tundra LT
Overall length	95.3in	99.6in	113in
Overall width	33.3in	33.3in	33.3in
Approx. weight	295/324lb	328lb	358lb
Ski stance	28.5in	28.5in	28.5in
Fuel capacity	6.9 US gal	6.9 US gal	6.9 US gal
Track width	15in	15in	15in
Track length	102.4in	124in	139in
Bore	72mm	72mm	72mm
Stroke	61mm	61mm	61mm
Displacement	248.2cc	248.2cc	248.2cc
Carburetor	VM 34	VM 34	VM 34
Horsepower	22hp	22hp	22hp

the more conventional torque reaction slide suspension and external, sprocket drive tracks.

1986-1994
★
Citation, Tundra and Tundra II models

1986

Changes were minor for 1986. A new hood material, Metton, was used. Like urethane, it was molded using the reaction injection molding technique. The material was more rigid and had a harder, smoother surface, producing a better finish. The LS/E model had a white hood while the other LS and the Tundras remained yellow.

A new ski with two forward spring mounting positions was used and changes were made to the inner half of the drive pulley to reduce its starting ratio.

1987

A third Tundra model was added for 1987. The machine was identical to the Tundra LT except it lacked oil injection. It was called the Tundra LTS and like the Tundra LT for 1987, it was fitted with an orange, polyethylene hood. The Tundra and the Citation LS had yellow, polyethylene hoods and the Citation LS/E had a white polyethylene hood.

All three Tundra models were equipped with square shaft clutches for the first time. The Citation models continued using the round-shaft roller clutch design.

A large cargo rack was standard fair on the Tundra LT with its 15x139in track. *Snow Goer Magazine*

For 1993, the Tundra II and Tundra II LT were fitted with a telescoping front suspension system. *Snow Goer Magazine*

1988

The Tundra LTS was dropped from the line and the chaincase on all the Tundra and Citation models was changed to accept a new brake caliper and eliminate oil spillage. Color became the single biggest change for the season with a bright red hood for the Citation LS, a burgundy hood on the LSE, yellow for the Tundra, and orange on the utility oriented Tundra LT. All chassis and belly pans remained black.

1989

The Citation LS and LSE were renamed the Safari Citation while the Tundra and Tundra LT were grouped with the utility sleds. Both Safari Citation models had a red hood and both Tundras were orange. The Citation models had a new design track which remained an internal drive type. Technical changes were minor for the season.

1990

Skis on the two Tundra models were reinforced with a vertical steel strap on its outer edge. Because the reinforcement was on one side of the ski only, there was a left and right ski. Little else changed for 1990.

1991

It was fitting for the Citation and Citation E to finish their run in the Ski-Doo line as Citation models, not Safari Citation models. For their final year, both models were dressed in white. Few other changes were made to the machines for the season.

The Tundra and Tundra LT also used the white hood. Both models were produced nearly unchanged for 1991 and 1992.

1993

The Tundra II and Tundra II LT continued as utility sleds in the Ski-Doo line. The major changes in them over their predecessors was the use of an updated type 277, radial fan-cooled engine and a new telescoping front suspension. The 277 engine was quite similar to the one used in Citation 3500. It was equipped with electronic ignition and oil injection. Both models were fitted with a square-shaft, two roller clutch. The basic "Citation" hood shape continued to be used with reliefs at the sides for the wider-stance, IFS suspension.

1994

For 1994, the square-shaft clutch was replaced with a Power Bloc design. Other changes made to the Tundra II and LT version were minor. Only the Tundra II LT with its 139in long will be built for 1995.

Tundra II and Tundra II LT		
	Tundra II	Tundra II LT
Overall length	106.7in	112in
Overall width	37.6in	37.6in
Approx. weight	335lb	355lb
Ski stance	32in	32in
Fuel capacity	6.9 US gal	6.9 US gal
Track width	15in	15in
Track length	124in	139in
Bore	72mm	72mm
Stroke	66mm	66mm
Displacement	268.7cc	268.7cc
Carburetor	VM 34	VM 34

The Safari

1984 Safari models and SS-25			
	Safari 377/E	Safari 447/GL	SS-25
Overall length	105in	110in	105in
Overall width	38in	38in	38in
Approx. weight	390/429lb	402/429lb	422lb
Ski stance	32.3in	32.3in	32.3in
Fuel capacity	7.6 US gal	7.6 US gal	7.6 US gal
Track width	15in/16.5in	16.5in	15in
Track length	114in	124in	114in
Bore	62mm	67.5mm	69.5mm
Stroke	61mm	61mm	61mm
Displacement	368.3cc	436.6cc	462.8cc
Carburetor	VM 34	VM 34	VM 34
Horsepower	38hp	44hp	54hp

1984

Ski-Doo's 25th anniversary was celebrated with the introduction of the Safari series, the flagship of which was the SS-25. An all-new chassis was used which had an aluminum tunnel mounted to a steel forward frame section with tubular steel cross member. Belly pans were made of Surlyn plastic. The hoods of the four Safari models were made of polycarbonate while the SS-25 had a fiberglass hood. Both hoods utilized a Surlyn nose cone which was a somewhat flexible material much like polyethylene. The nose cone covered the steel bumper when the hood was closed and had openings on the lower side that allowed you to pick the machine up by the bumper.

The air-cooled Safari models had a duct in the top of the hood that collected the cooling air from the engine and ducted it to louvers behind the windshield on the left side of the hood. It offered a convenient way to warm cold hands and defog glasses and face shields.

All the fuel tanks for the new line were designed to accept sensors for an electric fuel gauge but only the SS-25 was equipped with the gauge as standard equipment.

The new design paid a lot of attention to the fit and finish of the entire machine. A console joined the fuel tank to the hood, the rubber handlebar pad flowed from the console over the handlebars, the seat joined the fuel tank in a graceful curve, even the running boards joined the rear of the tunnel with a curved stamping, and on the Grand Luxe model, even more elegant end caps completed the transition. The Safari model's hoods had a retractable headlight while the SS-25's was recessed into the hood and fixed in position. The Safari was a graceful, beautifully detailed, elegant-looking machine. So outstanding was the overall package that Design Canada awarded its gold medal to the Safari in 1985.

The Safari, offered with a 377 or 447 engine, was totally new for 1984. Its sleek good looks de-manded the return of the retractable headlight. *Snow Goer Magazine*

There were four Safari models plus the SS-25 offered for 1984. The Safari 377 was offered in manual and electric start and was fitted with a 114in long track as was the SS-25. The track on the electric start version of the 377 was 16 1/2in wide while the manual start 377 and SS-25 had a 15in wide track. Safari 447 and Grand Luxe, which was an electric start version of the 447 with all the accessories, used a longer tunnel and a 124x16 1/2in track. All tracks were the conventional, external-drive type.

The suspension system was called the TRS6, which stood for Torque Reaction Suspension with 6in of movement. Ski suspension was handled by a single tapered leaf spring with hydraulic shock absorber.

A cast aluminum driven pulley mounted on the chaincase. No jackshaft was used. The brake disk mounted on the fixed half of the driven pulley, and a cable-operated, self-adjusting mechanical caliper handled stopping. A two-roller, square-shaft clutch was used on the air-cooled models while the liquid-cooled SS-25 was fitted with a three-roller square-shaft clutch with replaceable ramps. A steel damper ring was fastened to the fixed half of the SS-25's clutch. The additional mass helped dampen angular vibrations in the crankshaft.

The type 377 engine was almost identical to the one used on the Scandic and previously on the Citation 4500. The Safari version, however, was fitted with a fan-forced muffler system. The 447 was a new engine based on the 377 design. You had to look at the serial number tag to tell the two engines apart. A new, type 462, liquid-cooled, rotary valve engine was used in the SS-25. The new engine was a lightweight, compact version of the type 464 engine that had been used in the liquid-cooled Everest. A single, extruded aluminum heat exchanger mounted in the top of the tunnel of the SS-25. All three engines were equipped with oil injection, Nippon Denso electronic ignition and a single Mikuni VM 34 carburetor.

1985-1994
★↗
Safari and "spun-off" models

1985

The SS-25 became part of the new Formula series as the Formula SS. Four Safari models were produced for 1985. The Safari 377 and its electric start version returned virtually unchanged from 1984 as did the Safari 447 which was offered only in a manual start version. Safari Grand Luxe was fitted with a type 532, liquid-cooled, rotary valve engine. The 532 was a detuned, single-carburetor version of the type 537 engine used in the Formula. Rotary valve timing and exhaust and transfer port timing were much milder on the 532 than on the 537. The 532 produced about 60hp at 7000rpm while the 537 was making around 90hp at 7800rpm. Two extruded aluminum heat exchangers were fitted to the top of the tunnel for the Grand Luxe. Standard equipment on the GL included; electric starter, speedometer, tachometer, coolant temperature gauge, and halogen head lamp.

Named for Ski-Doo's 25th anniversary, the SS-25 was powered by the lightweight, liquid-cooled type 462 engine in 1984. *Snow Goer Magazine*

All Safari models were fitted with a black, polycarbonate hood in 1985.

1986

The Safari line up returned with minor changes for 1986 but with a lot more color. Both 377s got a yellow hood while the 447 was fitted with a red hood, and the Grand Luxe was given a rich, burgundy hood.

A new rear suspension system, which had been used the season before on the Formula SP, was installed on the Grand Luxe. It was a shorter movement version of the system used on the Blizzard MX. It offered about 8in of movement and made for a very comfortable ride. Like the MX and SP versions of the suspension, the two shock absorbers controlling the rear arm mounted vertically on each side of the tunnel, enclosed with polyethylene covers.

The Grand Luxe was fitted with an electric fuel gauge for 1986.

1987

The Safari 447 and Grand Luxe mutated into the Stratos and Escapade for 1987. Those two models are discussed in chapter 13. The Safari 377 and it's electric start version received minor updating. Most significant was use of the 16 1/2in-wide track on the manual start 377. A speedometer and electric fuel gauge became standard equipment for both 377s making them an even better bargain.

Scandic was reborn as a derivation of the Safari. A longer tunnel housing a 16 1/2x139in track was fitted and a passenger backrest and cargo rack were standard equipment. The new model was given the red hood from the previous season's Safari 447. Power came from the reliable type 503 fitted with a single VM 34 carburetor, oil injection and a fan-forced muffler. A high windshield and speedometer were standard equipment on the new Scandic.

1988

The 377 was again offered in manual and electric start versions with very few changes made. The Scandic name disappeared again as the long track model was renamed the Safari 503. It was joined by a similar model with

A stretched version of the Safari chassis was equipped with a 16.5x139in track and powered by the venerable type 503 engine. The long-track version was introduced as the Scandic 503 in 1987. Shown here is the 1988 version, then named the Safari 503. The machine was renamed the Safari Cheyenne for 1989. *Snow Goer Magazine*

reverse gear, appropriately named the Safari 503 R. The reversing chaincase was a planetary design similar to the one first used on the original Scandic R in 1984. The new version of the reversing chaincase had no neutral position, eliminating the need for a brake on the drive axle. The drive pulley on the 503s was Bombardier's new TRA design, first used on the Formula Plus.

A new, articulating suspension system was used on the R. It was basically one-half of the system used on the new Alpine II. The rear 12in of the rails attached with a pivot to the rest of the rail. If an obstacle was hit when backing up, the rear idlers could raise up about 6in allowing the track to form a 20-degree "attack angle" at the

A totally new, A-arm independent front suspension was developed for the 1990 Safari models. The system offered 7in of vertical travel and an extremely comfortable ride. *J-A Bombardier Museum*

rear of the track. An angled heel was added to the skis to allow for backing up.

1989

Marketing strategy for 1989 grouped eight models under the Safari name including two Citation models, the Stratos and the Escapade. Four of the models were based on the original Safari chassis. The 377 and its electric start version returned, renamed the Safari Scout. About the only change to the machine was the loss of its electric fuel gauge which was given to its new relative, Safari Saga. The Saga was similar to the Scout in all ways except for the use of the "SP" long travel rear suspension, a burgundy rather than yellow hood and the electric fuel gauge.

Not excluded from the name game, the Safari 503R was renamed the Safari Cheyenne. Only the "R" version was produced for 1989. Technical changes to the sled were minor.

1990

The Scout was offered only as a manual start model. The Cheyenne had a new rear arm on the track suspension to reduce weight transfer when pulling heavy loads and it was fitted with a new reversing chaincase that was used on the Escapade model in 1989. The new design placed the planetary gear components at the bottom of the chaincase at drive axle level, lowering the center of gravity of the design.

A totally new series of Safari models was introduced for 1990. The brand new chassis sported a transverse "A" arm or wishbone independent front suspension with 7in of vertical travel. Six models of the new design were produced. The smallest was powered by the venerable, type 377 engine and was available with or without electric start. They were named the Safari L and Safari LE. The type 447 engine returned to power the Safari LX and LXE, this time with dual, 34mm carburetors. The Safari GLX and LC mounted the type 467, rotary valve, liquid-cooled engine. This engine was similar to the Formula MX's but in a milder state of tune. It should not be confused with the type 462 engine used in the earlier Formula SS and SP.

The new chassis used an aluminum tunnel with a steel front section. All the new models were fitted with a 16 1/2x124in tracks. The track was a conventional, sprocket-drive design. Track suspension was a variation of the "SP" design with a single rear arm shock mounted inboard and offering 8.5in of travel.

The ski suspension reflected many nuances of a Formula I automobile suspension. The dumbbell shaped ski legs were forged with two spheres on them. Each sphere was the ball of a ball socket joint. A plastic socket at the end of each "A" arm accepted the spheres on the ski leg, allowing the ski leg to rotate for steering and maintain its camber angle through the suspension's travel. Transversely positioned shock absorbers mounted at the center of the chassis and to the upper "A" arm. During cornering, left and right sides were allowed to borrow spring pressure from each other through a stabilizer bar. The system provided a very comfortable ride and was quite light.

Driven pulleys were chaincase-mounted and equipped with a self-adjusting, mechanical disk brake. The Safari GLX model used a reversing chaincase with the planetary gears at the drive axle level similar to the Cheyenne's. All models used the TRA clutch.

A two-piece hood was used on all models. The lower portion of the hood was made of RIM Metton while the dark gray upper portion was made of polyethylene. The new Safari models were a colorful lot with a yellow hood on the L, a light gray hood on the LE, raspberry was the color for both LX models, dark gray was used on the GLX, and the LC was finished in bright red. The hood for the air-cooled models included an air duct

The Scandic II, with its 16.5x139in track, utilized the new Safari IFS suspension in 1992. *J-A Bombardier Museum*

A 503 engine powered the 1993 Safari Rally. *J-A Bombardier Museum*

which collected the cooling air from the engine and ducted it out through the left and right sides of the hood. The headlights mounted in the upper portion of the hood in a fixed position. The headlight lens was angled to match the windshield.

A speedometer was standard on the L and LE while the LX and LXE were equipped with a speedometer, tachometer, and electric fuel gauge. The GLX and LC came fully equipped with speedometer, tachometer, electric fuel gauge, and engine coolant temperature gauge. Handlebar heaters were standard equipment on the GLX and LC.

A high/low, two-up seat with backrest was used on the GLX along with right and left side saddle bags. A two-passenger seat was an option for the other Safari models. Another nice touch on the luxury oriented GLX were side moldings that functioned as footrests for the passenger. All versions utilized a polyethylene belly pan. Small snow deflectors or "flat wings" were made of polyethylene and bolted to the outside of the belly pan just behind the openings for the suspension. Snow kicked up by the skis and suspension was deflected away from the rider by these devices.

1991

It was the final year for the Cheyenne and virtually no changes were made to it. The Scout would survive unchanged for another year as a 1992 model. It would be the final use of the original Safari chassis design.

A lot of updating and recalibrating was done to the IFS Safari models for 1991. All the hoods received "NACA" type air inlet ducts. The air-cooled models had a single inlet added at the right side of the hood to feed the engine cooling fan while the liquid-cooled models had a duct added to both sides of the hood to lower underhood temperatures. The LE's hood remained yellow while the electric start version was painted magenta. Both LX models had a dark blue, metallic finish. "Mulberry", sort of a lavender color, was given the GLX and the LC's red hood was painted black for 1991.

The front frame was reinforced where the "A" arms attached at the bottom of the frame and steering stops were added at the steering arms.

A new twelve-pole, CDI system built by Ducati for Rotax was used for the first time on the two air-cooled engines. The system produced 160ws at 12v for lighting and featured a separate trigger or pulser coil for timing. Dual VM 30 carbs were fitted on the 337 engine and a new, single fuel pump was used on both the 377 and 447 engines.

The Safari LC had become Safari LCE for 1991 as electric start became standard equipment.

1992

The Safari LX and LXE with their 447 engines left the line for 1992 but the Skandic name returned as Skandic II in a standard and reverse version. Skandic was always a name associated with deep snow capabilities and the latest version was to be no exception with its 16.5x139in track. The two Skandic II models were powered by the same twin carb 377 that was used on the Safari L and LE.

The new Skandic II's slide rail design was not the articulating type used on the Cheyenne. A single aluminum rail ran the full length of the slider shoes. A cargo rack was standard on the long track Skandic IIs. A front molding was added to the top of the hood. The high windshield rounded out the new IFS utility sled.

A white hood was used on the Safari L while the Safari LE had a rose quartz hood. The LC got a metallic black hood while the GLX retained its Mulberry color, and both Scandic IIs were fitted with black hoods.

1993

The Safari GLX and LC were dropped from the line for 1993 while the Safari L returned almost unchanged and the LE was renamed the Safari DL (Deluxe). A new model called the Safari Rally was added. It utilized the same chassis and track as the L and DL but was powered by a type 503 engine with twin 34mm carburetors and a single tuned exhaust system. The air-cooled Safari models had all used a fan-forced muffler until the Rally came along. Its exhaust system was much like a Formula's system. It incorporated a "Y" pipe which led to a single tuned expansion chamber emptying into an after muffler. No fan cooling of the chamber or after muffler was employed.

All three Safari models had speedometers and heated hand grips. The Rally and DL had a tachometer as well as speedometer. The front molding on top of the hood that was used on the previous year's Scandic II was used on the three Safari models for 1993. The same high/low, two-up seat was used on the three Safari models. Only the Deluxe was equipped with electric start.

Four Scandic IIs, based on the IFS Safari design, were released for 1993. The 377 engine was used in a reverse and standard model of the Scandic II. Both Scandic II models powered by the 503 engine were equipped with the planetary design, reversing chaincase. One Scandic powered by the 503 engine was referred to as simply the 503 R. The other 503 powered Scandic was called the 503 R SLT. With its 15x156in long track, I can't imagine that SLT stood for anything other than: Super Long Track! The R SLT's track was an internal-drive type. Other Scandic II models used a conventional sprocket driven, 16.5x139in track. All Scandic II models were equipped with handlebar heaters and a speedometer.

Blue was the hood color for the three Safari models and the Scandic models were black.

1994

Other than cosmetic changes, little, other than adding electric start as standard equipment on the Rally, was done to the three Safari models. It was the final year for the Safari and its "A" arm front suspension.

Like the Safari models, the four "A" arm, IFS Scandic models had their final production run as 1994 models. There were no significant changes. Unlike the Safari name, however, the Scandic name would return on three new sleds for 1995.

"IFS" Safari models				
	L/LE	LX/LXE	GLX	LC
Overall length	109in	109in	106in	109in
Overall width	40.5in	40.5in	40.5in	40.5in
Approx. weight	450/469	456/483lb	558lb	516lb
Ski stance	36.3in	36.3in	36.3in	36.3in
Fuel capacity	7.5 US gal	9.5 US gal	9.5 US gal	9.5 US gal
Track width	16.5in	16.5in	16.5in	16.5in
Track length	124in	124in	124in	124in
Bore	62mm	67.5mm	69.5mm	69.5mm
Stroke	61mm	61mm	61mm	61mm
Displacement	368.3cc	436.5cc	462.8cc	462.8cc
Carburetor	VM 34	2 VM 34	VM 34	VM 34

In 1993 a 503 powered version of the Scandic II was first made available. Shown here is the 1994, Scandic II 503R. *Bombardier Corp.*

Chapter 13

The Stratos and Escapade

1987

The upper end of the original Safari line was replaced by the Stratos and Escapade models for 1987. These two models were adaptations of the Safari chassis. From the driver's footrests back, the new models were Safari. The hood, belly pan, engine, and front suspension were all new.

Central to the models was a new, telescoping front suspension system named Posi-Steer Suspension (PSS). The design separated the steering function from the suspension function so that no bump steer, scrub, castor, or camber angle change was possible. The widened cross member, 36.3in ski stance supported the suspension with a cylinder welded to each end. A cast aluminum cylinder with a lever arm was the steering arm of the design. It rode in bushings at the ends of the cross member and handled the steering function. It could only rotate in its bushings. There was no vertical motion of the arm so there could be no displacement of the tie rods with resulting bump steer.

The center of the steering arm had a square hole through which it supported the square-shafted ski leg. The square shape was used to transfer steering torque to the ski leg

1987 Stratos and Escapade		
	Stratos	Escapade
Overall length	105.5in	110.6in
Overall width	41.7in	41.7in
Approx. weight	419lb	474lb
Ski stance	36.3in	36.3in
Fuel capacity	7.6 US gal	7.6 US gal
Track width	16.5in	16.5in
Track length	114in	124in
Bore	72mm	72mm
Stroke	61mm	61mm
Displacement	496.5cc	496.5cc
Carburetor	2 VM 34	2 VM 34

from the steering arm as the ski leg was allowed to travel vertically. A shock adapter secured the hydraulic shock absorber to the bottom of the ski leg. A bracket off the cross member held the other end of the shock absorber. Left and right sides were linked with a stabilizer bar. The design offered 5in of vertical travel at the ski.

The track suspension was similar to the torque reaction system formerly used on the Formula SP, and was employed on the Safari Saga for 1987. It mounted twin shock absorbers for the rear arm vertically on the outside of the tunnel. The system offered about 8in of travel. The Stratos mounted a 16.5x114in track while the Escapade used a 16.5x124in track.

A new, polyethylene belly pan fully enclosed the front of the machine and offered a broad, smooth surface to the snow, making the machines quite good in deep snow. The

The hood and windshield of the 1987 Stratos and Escapade models were designed to add heated air from the engine to the air flowing around the rider. A duct through the hood in front of the windshield allowed the air to flow around the base of the windshield to the rider(s). *Bombardier Corp.*

hood and windshield worked together in accomplishing what was called the "heat-flow" cab. The windshield, which was fixed to the hood, curved in at its base where it met the hood. This provided a channel between the hood and windshield that wrapped around the windshield to the rider. Heated air from the engine was exhausted into the channel in front of the windshield and allowed to flow around the windshield to mix with the oncoming air and warm the air surrounding the rider.

The hood was made of RIM Metton and the original windshields were made of a single molding of clear polycarbonate. The windshield was a complex shape, and to provide the necessary strength of the one-piece design, the thickness of the windshield varied from top to bottom. A replacement wind-

shield with a smoked bottom portion was later offered. The Stratos' hood was painted blue, while the Escapade's was black with gold pinstriping.

Power was supplied by a type 503 engine pumped up with the use of a new expansion chamber exhaust system and twin 34mm carburetors. The exhaust system used a "Y" pipe to feed the twin cylinders to a single expansion chamber. The chamber emptied into a separate after muffler. The chamber was not cooled with the fan-forced muffler design.

Both machines were equipped with electric fuel gauges, handlebar heaters, speedometers, and tachometers. Electric start and a hi/low, two-up seat were standard on the Escapade only. A small number of electric start Stratos units were built late in production. They were identified with a hood decal striped in blue, white and gray.

1988

The electric start version of the Stratos officially joined the manual start Stratos and the Escapade. A two-piece windshield now used a black polycarbonate base with a clear polycarbonate sheet attached to it. The two Stratos models retained their blue hoods while the Escapade's hood was painted maple red.

1989

The 1989 name game grouped the Escapade with the Safari models as the Safari Escapade and changed the Stratos' name to Voyageur, calling it the Safari Voyageur. Electric start was standard on both the Escapade and the Voyageur. A new reversing chaincase playing on the design of the Scandic R's was added to the Escapade . The new chaincase moved the planetary gear system to the bottom of the chaincase, lowering the center of gravity. Bombardier's new progressive throttle was added to both machines. Two different shades of gray were used on the hoods for 1989. It was the final year of the Escapade and Voyageur and their PSS suspension.

1989 was the final year for the Stratos, whose name had been changed to Voyageur for 1989, and Escapade, and the last Ski-Doo models, along with the Safari Saga of the same year, to use a version of the Blizzard 5500 MX suspension that mounted the rear shock absorbers outside the tunnel. *Bombardier Corp.*

Chapter 14

The Formula Series

1984-1985 ★★★★★	Formula Pro-Stock

1985	
★★	SS
★★★⤴	SP
★★★	Formula MX
★★	Formula Plus

1985

The Formula series included four models for 1985. Two machines, the Formula SS and SP, were based on the Safari chassis and used a conventional, leaf spring ski suspension.

The Formula SS had been seen in 1984 as the SS 25. Twin heat exchangers were installed to increase cooling capacity but little else was changed on the Formula SS when compared

While the big news for 1985 was the PRS-suspended Formula MX and Formula Plus, the SS- 25 of the previous season returned and was renamed the Formula SS. *Bombardier Corp.*

The 1985 Formula SP was essentially identical to the Formula SS with the exception of its shorter travel version of the Blizzard 5500 MX rear suspension. *Snow Goer Magazine*

to its predecessor. A mid-season introduction of the Formula SP introduced what became known as the "SP" suspension. The new track suspension system was a shorter travel version of the system used on the Blizzard 5500 MX. It had 8in of vertical travel and offered a superb ride. The suspension system was characterized by the two shock absorbers that mounted on the outside of the tunnel at the rear of the machine. The rest of the machine was identical to the Formula SS with exception of its white hood.

The Ski-Doo dealer network had waited anxiously for the other two Formula models for 1985, the Formula MX and Formula Plus. Bombardier had developed many different prototype IFS sleds through the years and had produced the very successful systems used on the racing Blizzard models. Plans were finally made to produce the two 1985 Formula models using what was called the Progressive Reaction Suspension system (PRS). The design utilized bell cranks in the ski and track suspension systems that varied the rate of compression of the shocks and springs in the system based on the position of the suspension components. The suspension compressed more easily during its first inches of movement than its final inches of movement, giving the system a true, rising rate with 6in of travel at the ski and at the rear arm of the track suspension.

Many of the components and concepts used in the suspension design had been worked out on sno-cross race tracks in previous seasons by Gerard Karpik and Brad Hul-

1985 Formula Series			
	SS	SP	MX	Plus
Overall length	105in	105in	107in	107in
Overall width	38in	38in	41in	41in
Approx. weight	423lb	434lb	438lb	448lb
Ski stance	32.3in	32.3in	36.3in	36.3in
Fuel capacity	7.6 US gal	7.6 US gal	10.9 US g	10.9 US gal
Track width	15in	16.5in	15in	16.5in
Track length	114in	114in	114in	114in
Bore	69.5mm	69.5mm	69.5mm	72mm
Stroke	61mm	61mm	61mm	64mm
Displacement	462.8cc	462.8cc	462.8cc	521.2cc
Carburetor	VM 34	VM 34	2 VM 34	2 VM 40

ings. The pair was incredibly successful on the race courses and plans were made to produce a version of the sled for qualified sno-cross racers. In-house, the project was called Formula MX. One hundred of the IFS sleds were produced with a twin-shock rear arm suspension as 1984 models. A quantity of fifty were built with a single-shock rear suspension arm as 1985 models. These race sleds carried the Formula MX name and much of what became technology used on the first Formula models. The 150 sno-cross race sleds displayed the Ski-Doo brand name on the sides of the hood, "Formula MX" across the nose of the hood, and the model name, "Pro-Stock", for the class in which it was qualified to race, was on the front suspension swing arms. The 1984 and 1985 Pro-Stocks are among the rarest Ski-Doos ever produced.

The Formula MX and Plus utilized a tubular steel front frame section and an aluminum tunnel. A RIM urethane belly pan was used along with a fiberglass hood. The steel front bumper was concealed behind a urethane front nose cone that attached to the hood. Silver was the hood color for the Formula Plus and the MX was given classic Ski-Doo yellow.

The shock absorbers for the front suspension were mounted in line with the frame in the nose of the sled. A rocker or bell crank mounted to the rear end of the shock and a drop link connected the other end of the bell crank to the lower radius rod. The bell crank provided the rising rate to the system. The sets of dual radius rods connected to a swing arm that pivoted at the outside of the frame by the rider's feet. A stabilizer bar mounted beneath the belly pan connected the left and right swing arms.

Formula SP models signified a major step in the development of high-performance production models, so they're becoming quite collectible.

The track suspension system mounted a single shock absorber and spring to the front arm through a rocker mechanism, and two horizontally mounted shocks with coil springs controlled the rear arm. The two rear shocks mounted to levers on the rear arm that provided the rising rate. A shackle linked the rear arm to the slide rails. While both models used conventional, sprocket-driven tracks, the Plus had a 16.5in wide track and the MX was fitted with a 15in track.

Predecessor to the Formula Plus and MX in 1985 were the 1984 Formula MX Pro Stock snow cross race sleds. One hundred Pro Stocks were built as 1984 models and fifty were built as 1985 models, placing them among the rarest Ski-Doos built. *Gerard Karpik*

A jackshaft carried the driven pulley on the left side of the chassis, connecting it to the chaincase mounted on the opposite side of the chassis. Brakes were self adjusting mechanical types with the disk mounted on the right side of the jackshaft. Ski-Doo had used silent chain or timing chain in the chaincase on their race sleds previously but the 1985 Formula Plus and MX were the first "consumer" sleds so equipped. Both the MX and Plus used a three-ramp, square-shaft clutch and new, cast aluminum driven pulley.

Power for the MX came from a type 467 Rotax, a new version of the 462.8cc, type 464 engine. The engine had dual 34mm carbs, oil injection, a single tuned expansion chamber with after muffler, and was a rotary valve, liquid-cooled twin. The Plus powered up with a type 537 Rotax, a heated-up version of the type 534 used in the Blizzard 9700. It too used a single tuned expansion chamber with after muf-

fler and was fitted with dual 40mm carbs and oil injection. Ignition for both engines was Nippon Denso CDI with a 160w lighting coil.

The engines were mounted to the chassis using a new technique. Rather than using a plate under the engine, four mounts were attached at mid-point on the crankcase. It allowed the engine to be mounted lower in the chassis, clutch alignment was more constant and vibration levels were reduced. It is one of the reasons the IFS Formula models always felt so smooth. A torque rod attached under the engine in the front left corner.

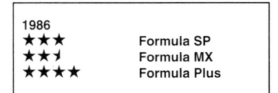

1986
★★★ Formula SP
★★☆ Formula MX
★★★★ Formula Plus

1986

As the Formula SS was dropped from the series, the Formula MX long-track was added with a 16.5x124in track. The Formula SP had attracted a growing following and was continued almost unchanged for 1986. The most significant improvement made to the 1986 Formula models was the use of Bombardier's new, Total Range Adjustable clutch (TRA) on the Formula Plus. The clutch was a joint design effort between Bombardier-Rotax in Gunskirchen, Austria, and Bombardier, Valcourt. The clutch was produced by Rotax in Austria.

The design incorporated a larger diameter than previous clutches, which meant the driven pulley had to open to a smaller diameter to maintain proper belt tension. The clutch would actually shift to a 1.1:1 overdrive ratio. The large amount of ratio change in the design was what the "total range" portion of its name referred to.

Chaincase gearing was lowered from 26/38 in 1985 to 20/38 with the TRA equipped 1986 Plus. Another feature of the clutch was its simple adjustability. The three ramps in the clutch pivoted on the end closest the center of the clutch. The outer end rested on an eccentric bolt that could be rotated through six adjustment positions, changing the height of the ramp and the shift speed of the clutch. Adjustments could be performed without taking the clutch apart. The adjustment had no effect on engagement speed but each increase in adjustment position resulted in about a 200rpm increase in the top rpm of the engine. The adjustable shift speed accounted for the "adjustable" portion of its name.

The TRA clutch is now used on almost all of Ski-Doo's models and, from the very first year on the 1986 Formula Plus, has proven to be dependable, consistent in its performance, lubrication free, requires extremely little maintenance, and provides superb drive belt life.

The 1985 Formula Plus had a strong resemblance to the Pro Stock race sled. Here its sleek good looks and silver color are compared to a silver Ferrari 912 Boxer. *Lance Parthe*

The belly pan openings for the suspension were made taller for 1986 and the new RIM Metton hoods had no separate nose cone. The reliefs for the suspension were also made higher on the new hoods. A black hood was used on the Plus while the MX retained its yellow color. The aluminum tunnel of both sleds remained black. Other changes were minor, such as the addition of ventilation holes in the recoil starter on the Formula MX and Plus.

1987

The Formula SP was dropped from the line for 1987, leaving only the three IFS Formula models in the series. The most startling changes to the Formula sleds for 1987 were their colors. A red belly pan, chassis, and hood made the Formula Plus instantly recognizable. Only the wide white stripes on the hood and the chassis and the black seat

broke up the brilliant red machine. The Formula MX and MX LT got silver hoods with blue stripes while their chassis and belly pans remained black.

Kevlar cord was added to the Formula Plus track and the belly pans for all three Formula models were made of polyethylene. A fuel shut-off valve was added to eliminate the possibility of fuel leaking into the crankcase while trailering the sleds. The MX models were fitted with a new coolant reservoir to allow the use of a "T" fitting in the hose from the thermostat. The new arrangement allowed a portion of the engine coolant to bypass the heat exchangers and *increase* the engine operating temperature. The MX engine

Bombardier chose to introduce their all-new Total Range Adjustable (TRA) clutch on the 1986 Formula Plus. The TRA combined with the fantastic type 537 engine was an astounding success and the TRA clutch now shifts for all but the smallest Ski-Doos. *J-A Bombardier Museum*

ran so cool it was hard to keep it running cleanly at low speeds and throttle settings. The increase in operating temperature helped clean up the bottom end response. The MXs were fitted with TRA clutches after the design's incredibly successful introduction on the Formula Plus in 1986.

1988

Tapered tunnels for 1988 gave the Formula models better performance in deep snow and a high-tech look as the twin rear shocks and their linkages were exposed. A new rear bumper could be installed in a high or low position, allowing the rider to set it up for his conditions and use. The ends of the new bumper were covered by a decorative polyethylene end cap. Growing environmental concerns led to the installation of coolant overflow tanks on the three Formula models.

Skis on all the IFS Formula sleds had been 4.6in wide until the 1988 Formula MX LT was fitted with 5.5in-wide skis. The long-track model was aimed at the deep snow areas of the West and the extra floatation of the wide skis was needed in those conditions. The bell crank or rocker arm of the front suspension was changed for 1988, lowering the machine in the front and reducing ski pressure. All Formula models were fitted with a high, 18in, windshield and the lower, 14in, windshield became an option. The Plus remained red and the MXs retained their silver hoods.

1989
★★↙
★★★   Formula MX, Plus and LT
★★★   Formula Mach I

1989

Two new Formula models joined the ranks in 1989, the Formula Plus LT and the exciting Formula Mach I which displaced the Formula Plus as the top of the line. The Formula MX and MX LT changed the least in 1989. Like all the Formula sleds, ski suspension springs with higher preloads were used to raise the front end and increase ski pres-

sure and Bombardier's new, progressive throttle control was fitted to the entire series.

A new type 536 engine was used in the two Plus models. The engine was a detuned version of the 537 engine. Cylinders with low, rectangular exhaust ports, dual 34mm carburetors and a shorter duration, "202" rotary valve created an engine with a very wide power curve, provided excellent fuel economy but produced less peak power than the type 537 engine. The Plus was given a 15x114in track and the new Plus LT had a 16.5x124in track. A new seat design for the Plus and Mach I covered the entire fuel tank.

Many new features debuted on the new Formula Mach I. The engine was the center of attention, a type 583 engine displacing 580.7cc. It was a liquid-cooled, rotary valve, oil-injected, twin-cylinder engine with RAVE exhaust valves. RAVE stands for Rotax Adjustable Variable Exhaust. Many thought the "A" in the acronym stood for Automatic but Rotax made it clear by casting the full name on the sides of the cylinders.

The RAVE valve is a guillotine type slide positioned at the top of the exhaust port. A spring, with adjustable preload, is used to hold the valve in its low position. A connec-

The 1987 Formula Plus' red paint job with white accent stripes really made it stand out on the snow and generated new excitement over the Plus. *J-A Bombardier Museum*

The Formula models were fitted with a tapered tunnel for 1988. The modification to the tunnel gave the Formula models a "high-tech" look and increased their performance in deep snow. *J-A Bombardier Museum*

1989 Formula Series			
	MX/LT	Plus/LT	Mach I
Overall length	109in	109in	109in
Overall width	41in	41in	41in
Approx. weight	489/513lb	505/518lb	517lb
Fuel capacity	10.8 US gal	10.8 US gal	10.8 US gal
Track width	15in/16.5in	15in/16.5in	16.1in
Track length	114in/124in	114in/124in	121in
Bore	69.5mm	72mm	76mm
Stroke	61mm	64mm	64mm
Displacement	462.8cc	521.2cc	580.7cc
Carburetor	2 VM 34	2 VM 34	2 VM 38

tion to the exhaust passage allows a diaphragm attached to the valve to sense the pressure in the exhaust passage. When the exhaust pressure is high enough, at higher speeds and throttle settings, the spring compresses and the valve slides to its highest position, effectively raising the height of the exhaust port and increasing its port timing. The patented design is wonderfully simple and allows the engine to produce gobs of low-speed power without sacrificing high peak power. Because most riding is done at part-throttle settings, the design also greatly improved fuel economy.

Bombardier-Rotax's RAVE valve design was first used on Bombardier's Can-Am motorcycle engines. The concept was first seen on a snowmobile engine in 1985 on Michel Gingras' Formula I, twin-track oval track race sled. Gingras proved the worth of the design by winning the Eagle River World Championship on his first time out with the new engine.

The Mach I used a single, tuned expansion chamber like the other Formula models. Twin 38mm carbs handled fuel delivery.

For the first time, an internal-drive, 16.1x121in track was used on a Formula. Tracks with four rows of drive lugs were considered standard on the 1989 Mach I but some Machs were produced with tracks with six rows of drive lugs. A single or mono shock rear arm suspension system was used, offering a plusher ride than the other Formula models. The Mach I was finished in black with white graphics.

<table>
<tr><td>1990
★★⌁
★★★</td><td>Formula models
Plus 500</td></tr>
</table>

1990

Nine Formula models were available as 1990 models. All nine models were equipped with internal-drive tracks with six rows of drive lugs. The standard models used a 16.1x121in track while the long-track models used a new 16.1x139in track. A mono shock rear arm, similar to the 1989 Mach's, was used on the track suspension of all models.

Long-track versions of the Formula MX and Plus were produced with a single passenger seat, and a separate long-track model was produced with a high/low, two-up seat with passenger backrest. The Formula Mach I was available in a long track version named the

Excitement over the Formula Mach I with its RAVE valve, 580.7cc engine, mono-shock rear suspension, and internal drive track had the new model sold out long before the winter of 1988-1989 began. *Snow Goer Magazine*

Formula Mach I XTC. (While the acronym suggests "ecstasy" it actually stood for Extra Traction and Comfort). Only a single-seat version of the XTC was produced. The extended tunnels of the long-track models was covered behind the seats with a polyethylene molding that also mounted the taillight assembly.

A new, two-piece cylinder head was used on the MX's 467 engine. The bottom casting contained the cylinder compression while the top casting formed the outer water jacket over the head. The new design allowed the head to be made using pressure die casting techniques.

Coolant reservoirs were replaced with a plastic fitting that joined the hoses and allowed filling of the system. The design was used to save weight.

While the other models had an electric fuel gauge, the MXs were given a sight gauge in the left side of the fuel tank. All Formula models received new steering arms and steering pivot arms to reduce bump steer at the top and bottom limits of suspension travel.

The ninth Formula model for 1990 was aimed at competition in the I-500 cross country race. Named the Formula Plus 500, the new model was powered by a type 536 engine fitted with 537 cylinders, a longer duration "207" rotary valve, and twin 38mm carburetors.

While most of the machine was standard issue Formula Plus, the 500's ski stance was widened to 39.8in and many components were reinforced for the rigors of cross country racing.

<table>
<tr><td>1991-1992
★★⌁
★★★⌁</td><td>Formula models
X versions</td></tr>
</table>

1991

Thirteen model numbers were initially issued for the Formula series in 1991 as electric start became a feature, and special competition versions of each Formula joined the line. Basic models of the MX and Plus returned

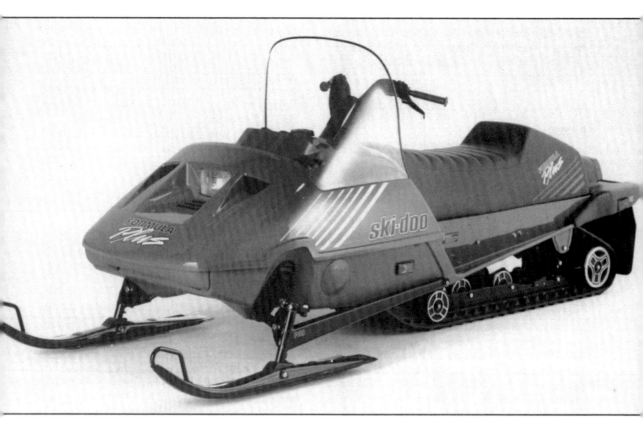

Pressure from the deep snow, mountain riders resulted in the introduction of the Formula Mach I XTC for 1990. A 16x139in internal-drive track provided the floatation and stretched the tunnel out, allowing space for a cargo rack. *J-A Bombardier Museum*

along with long-track models now called XTCs as was the long-track Mach I in 1990. Electric start versions of both the standard length machines and the XTC versions were produced, a first for the Formula family. In addition, a competition version of the MX and Plus were added, named the Formula MX X and the Formula Plus X. The Formula Mach I was not built in an electric start model but an optional electric start kit was available. An XTC, long-track model was made as was a Formula Mach I X. The battery for the electric start models was mounted on top of the tunnel, underneath the fuel tank. To make room for the battery a new, smaller fuel tank was used that carried 8.8 US gallons.

The XTC Formula models had two-up seats with a back rest and rear cargo racks. Riders from areas with deep snow such as the mountains and Alaska often crawl all around the machine as they traverse mountain sides and sashay through deep powder. A back rest and high rack can get in the way during this kind of maneuvering. Versions of the XTC were produced with single seats and a low rack for these areas, bringing the Formula model count up to eighteen for 1991.

The series received major restyling with an exciting new hood shape with an angled headlight lens and comfortable new seats. Colors remained unchanged on the new Machs and Pluses while the MX's hoods were painted in a beautiful pearl white. The windshield was made in three sections. A right and left side bubble offered wind protection for the hands and the windshield itself fastened to the two bubbles. A low, single-piece, opaque "windshield" was standard on the X models. All the Mach Is had handlebar heaters for the first time and a parking brake was added to all Formula models.

New power was given to the Mach I with the type 643 engine, which displaced 617cc. The RAVE and rotary valved engine was fitted with 40mm carburetors and dual fuel pumps. A "Y" pipe and single expansion chamber was used.

The driven pulley of all Formula models were fitted with "windage plates." These aluminum disks covered the reinforcing webs on the driven pulley halves, reducing drag created by pumping air with the webs.

A number of components changed in the front suspension to allow the use of a new attachment of the stabilizer bar to the swing arms. The former sliding plastic block connection was replaced with a short drop link arrangement.

The Mach I X and Plus X were aimed at drag and oval racing while the MX X was intended to compete under the new rules of the I-500 committee. Twin expansion chambers were fitted to the Mach I X. A "Y" adapter collected the exhaust at the end of the two pipes and fed it to a single after muffler. The type 643 engine was modified and fitted with two 44mm carburetors. The engine from the previous year's Plus 500 was used in the Plus X while the MX X used a standard type 467 engine.

All the "X" models' front frame sections were made of thin-gauge 4130 chrome-moly steel and had a ski stance of 39.8in. The suspension on the Plus and Mach "X"s remained quite standard but the MX X received a completely new rear suspension. The design linked the front and rear arms so that when the front arm contacted an obstacle, the rear arm raised also, eliminating much of the kick that could occur at racing speeds. Engan high-pressure gas shocks with remote reservoirs were used on the front suspension of the MX X.

1992

Electric start was offered as standard equipment only on the Plus E and Plus XTC E. The MX XTC came standard with a reversing chaincase. The chaincase was a new design, not the planetary system used on the Escapade. It was designed to be added as an accessory on all Formula models. Mach I XTCs

were produced in a single-seat version and two-up version with the a high/low seat. Touring on the constantly expanding trail systems was becoming increasingly popular and the larger, more powerful machines were catching on with touring enthusiasts. A Mach I X and Plus X brought the line of Formula models up to eleven for 1992. Graphics on all models were updated but the basic black, red and white remained on the hoods of the Formula models.

Ski stance on all the Formula models with 121in long tracks was set at 39.8in while the XTC versions remained at 36.3in to allow easier deep snow maneuvering. The sliding block connection of the stabilizer bar to the swing arms returned to the design used in 1990. Handlebar heaters became standard equipment on all Formula models.

A new rear suspension, the C-7, was used on all Formula models. A twin-shock rear arm, similar to the early Formula models, was employed along with high-pressure gas shocks.

The Formula Plus was fitted with a new type 582 engine, which was a toned down version of the type 583 engine previously used in the Mach I and used in the 1991 Plus

The Formula series received new styling for 1991 and an "X" version of each Formula aimed at competition. Here the Mach I X shows its muscle. *Snow Goer Magazine*

1992 Formula Series

	MX/XTCR	Plus/ XTC/X	Mach I/XTC/X
Overall length	109in/117in	109in/117in/109in	109in/117in/109in
Overall width	44in/42in	44in/42in/44.4in	44in/42in/44.4in
Approx. weight	521/580lb	535/574/540lb	551/583/560lb
Fuel capacity	9.3/9.3US gal	9.3/9.3/9.3US gal	9.3/9.3/9.3 US gal
Track width	16.1/16.1in	16.1/16.1/15in	16.1/16.1/15in
Track length	121/139in	121/139in/121in	121in/139in/121in
Bore	69.5mm	76mm	76mm/76mm/78mm
Stroke	61mm	64mm	68mm/68mm/70mm
Displacement	462.8cc	580.7cc	617cc/617cc/669cc
Carburetor	2-34	2-34/2-34/2-38	2-40/2-40/2-44

500. The 582 was a rotary valve, liquid-cooled twin but it was not equipped with RAVE Exhaust valves. Twin 34mm carbs were fed through a "508" rotary valve and a single tuned expansion chamber handled the outlet end. Only minor changes affected the Mach I and MX's engines. The metal coolant reservoir was put back on all Formula models after experiencing problems bleeding air from the cooling systems using the small plastic fitting.

The Plus X and Mach X used the standard Formula chassis for 1992 but it was fitted with a 15in wide track and adjustable sway bar that connected to the swing arms with a ball joint linkage. A RAVE valve 583 with twin 38mm carbs powered the Plus X while a new

type 670 engine with twin pipes powered the Mach I X.

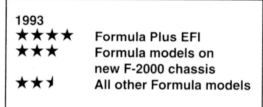

1993
★★★★ Formula Plus EFI
★★★ Formula models on new F-2000 chassis
★★↗ All other Formula models

Rating the collectability of newer models not possible at this time.

1993

Three models of the Formula MX were produced. The standard MX was the familiar single-person sled with a 121in track. A two-passenger version was also produced with the 121in track. The same two-passenger seat with backrest was used on the XTC R version with the 139in track. All three models were equipped with speedometer, tachometer, electric fuel gauge, and temperature gauge. Like all the Formula models for 1993, the MXs were fitted with heated hand grips and throttle handles (also called thumb warmers). The MX's engine changed little but was fitted with a 220w, twelve-pole Nippon Denso magneto.

There were six Formula Plus models offered in 1993. The type 582 engine returned with a new, two-piece cylinder head, similar to the MX's, and twin-circuit thermostat. Electric start was available only on the 121in track version of the Plus. Like the MX, a two-passenger seat was available on the 121in track and standard on the XTC.

XTC long-track models of the Plus and MX were available with an array of seat and cargo rack options for 1991. Shown here is the Formula Plus XTC with a two-up seat and large cargo rack. *Snow Goer Magazine*

1993 Formula MX Z and Mach I Z		
	Formula MX Z	**Formula**
Mach Z		
Overall length	110.2in	110.2in
Overall width	46in	46in
Approx. weight	470lb	530lb
Ski stance	40in	40in
Fuel capacity	11.1 US gal	11.1 US gal
Track width	15in	15in
Track length	121in	121in
Bore	69.5mm	69.5mm
Stroke	61mm	68mm
Displacement	462.8cc	774cc
Carburetor	2 VM 34	3 TM38

The Formula Plus X returned with its type 583 engine and was the only Formula that didn't run the new twelve-pole magneto. Other than a change from a "207" to a "504" rotary valve and installation of VM 38 carburetors, little else changed on either the engine or the chassis.

A new system was added to the standard Formula Plus to produce the Formula Plus EFI. The Electronic Fuel Injection system was a design produced by Mikuni for Bombardier-Rotax. All other EFI systems used on snowmobiles vary the duration of the injection pulse to control fuel flow. Mikuni's system used a pulse of fixed duration and varied the pressure at the injector to meet the engine's needs. The system required the use of a battery but almost all other features of the Plus EFI were the same as the standard Formula Plus.

A totally new version of the type 670 engine used in the previous year's Mach I X landed in the Mach Is for 1993. The engine had a single tuned pipe, VM 40 carbs, RAVE valves, a "500" rotary valve, and it made lots of horsepower! A two-up version of the Mach I was produced on the 121in track and the XTC, 139in track version also utilized the two-up seat.

A new concept Formula, the Formula Grand Touring, was introduced for 1993. The machine utilized the basic Formula chassis with a 16.1x121in track. Power came from a type 582 engine as used in the Formula Plus for 1993, and it was equipped with electric start and reverse.

The seat was wonderfully comfortable with an adjustable back rest for the passenger. Grab handles for the passenger were electri-

cally heated and behind the passenger was a handy cargo rack. The skis were Bombardier's new UHMW polyethylene skis that were also used on the new "Z" models. The handlebar and thumb warmer switches were very large and mounted in the center of the handlebar pad where they were easily switched with any part of a gloved hand. Dual rearview mirrors finished off the safety features. While the other Formula models retained their black, red, and white colors, the Grand Touring's hood was painted in a rich blue.

The big excitement for 1993 was the introduction of Ski-Doo's all-new, F-2000 chassis on the Formula Mach Z and Formula MX Z. The new chassis was all aluminum with a polyethylene belly pan. Controlling the UHMW polyethylene skis was a simplified system called Direct Shock Action (DSA). It was similar to the Super Stock Blizzard suspension of the late seventies where the shock attached directly to the swing arm without linkages and offered 7in of travel. At the rear was an improved C-7 suspension system with two high-pressure gas shocks controlling the rear arm and providing 7.5in of travel.

Ski stance was set at 40in and both models used a 15x121in. polyester cord-reinforced, internal-drive track. The driven pulley was jackshaft-mounted and a mechanical, self-adjusting disk brake was used.

The only Ski-Doo ever offered with electronic fuel injection was the 1993 Formula Plus EFI. *Snow Goer Magazine*

Growing interest in touring by snowmobile prompted the introduction of Ski-Doo's Grand Touring model for 1993. Heated hand grips and an adjustable backrest made the Grand Touring a real comfort for the passenger. *Bombardier*

A totally new, all-aluminum chassis with DSA suspension was used on the exciting Formula Mach Z and MX Z for 1993. Shown here is the Formula Mach Z, powered by a new, liquid-cooled, 774cc, triple-cylinder, reed valve Bombardier-Rotax engine. *Snow Goer Magazine*

The Formula MX Z was powered by a type 470 engine, a modified version of the type 467 engine. The engine mounted to the chassis with a plate under the engine. The cylinders were modified 467 cylinders and could be identified by the letter "Z" stamped beneath the name "Rotax," which was cast on the sides of the cylinders. The MX Z was finished with a yellow hood and black chassis, belly pan and seat.

A completely new three-cylinder engine powered the Mach Z. The engine featured reed valve induction rather than rotary valve, gear-driven water- and oil-injection pumps at the magneto end of the crankshaft, RAVE valves, three flat slide, Mikuni TM 38 carburetors, and three individually tuned expansion chambers emptying into a single muffler. Peak horsepower on the new triple occurred at 8550rpm. A Comet drive pulley was standard on the Formula Mach Z in 1993.

1994

As the original PRS Formula chassis was used on fewer models and the new F-2000 chassis with its DSA front suspension took over, the

"Formula" name was used less, in fact only three models carried the Formula name in 1994: the Formula ST, Formula STX (also made in a two-up version), and Formula Z. These sleds all had red hoods and were grouped as "sport-performance" sleds.

A type 467 engine powered the ST while the others all ran the RAVE-valved, type 583. The engine in the ST was the same engine used in the MX and MXZ, which was usually referred to in brochures as a type 470, which added to confusion. The 470 number probably evolved as a way to separate the 467 as used in the F-2000 chassis from the 467 as used in the original Formula chassis. Engine compartments became more colorful as cylinder heads were painted, usually to match the hood color of the machines.

The STX's 583 engine was fitted with 38mm carbs while the Formula Z had 40mm Mikunis. The rest of the engine was identical between the two models. The Z, however, had other features such as an electric fuel gauge, coolant temperature gauge, high-pressure gas shocks all around, adjustable stabilizer bar, plastic skis, and a low windshield.

The Mach I and Mach Z were grouped as "muscle sleds." The 1994 Mach I and Grand Touring models were the last machines to utilize the "original" Formula chassis design. Bullet proof and very powerful, the Mach I's type 670 engine received little more than a violet

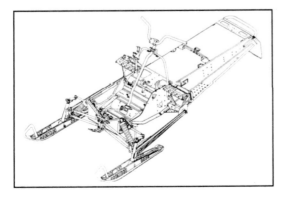

The F-2000, all-aluminum chassis was so named because it would take Ski-Doo into the year 2000. *Bombardier Corp.*

paint job for its cylinder head. Few updates were made to the Mach I.

So many changes were made to the type 779 triple used in the Mach Z that it was considered a new engine. The basic configuration remained unchanged but many of the glitches uncovered the previous season were corrected. The new version of the engine was equipped with a TRA clutch. The F-2000 chassis had proven to be very strong and few changes were made. RIM urethane was used as the hood material for 1994.

Three MX models were classified as "cross country" sleds, one of which, the MX Z X, was aimed at competition. All three models rode on the new, DSA chassis. While the MX used conventional gas shocks, the MX Z and MX Z X were fitted with Kayaba, rebuildable, high pressure gas shocks. An adjustable sway bar design was standard on the MX Z and MX Z X and the MX used a wide, steel ski while the MX Z and MX Z X were fitted with a narrow steel ski. For the first time since the oval-racing Blizzard models, hydraulic brakes again appeared on the MX Z and MX Z X. A Magura, handlebar-mounted master cylinder supplied a Wilwood caliper mounted on the chaincase.

The engines for all three models were type 467s. The MX and MX Z used the same version of the engine but the MX Z X had a modified version. A triple-exhaust port cylinder was used on the MX Z X and the casting showed that a RAVE exhaust port was in the future for the engine though it did not appear in 1994. The new cylinder was cast iron lined. A longer-duration rotary valve and different expansion chamber completed the differences between the engines.

The Grand Touring line expanded to three models, all of which were on the original Formula chassis design. A type 582 Rotax powered the Grand Touring and its long track XTC version. Other than the addition of the 16.1x139in track and larger cargo rack on the XTC version, little was changed from 1993.

Extra touring snap was added to the Grand Touring SE by bolting in the type 670 engine right out of the Mach I. The machine was equipped with electric start, reverse

The 1994 Mach I was the last Mach built on the original PRS-suspended chassis. Its RAVE-valved, 670cc engine provided plenty of power. *Bombardier Corp.*

Bombardier defined a machine for the mountain rider with the 1994 Summit. Its 15x136in deep-profile track, 36in ski stance, wide plastic skis, and HAC-equipped carburetors made it the way to travel in the mountains. Originally offered with a 583 and 470 engine, a mid-season introduction of the 670 was made for 1994. *Snow Goer Magazine*

gear, and unique, adjustable rear shocks. A screw setting allowed adjustment of the low-speed compression damping rate to match the load on the machine to the trail conditions. A 16.1x121in track was used and the machine had all the other comfort and convenience features of the other Grand Touring models.

The first spin-off of the new F-2000 chassis appeared as the Summit, offered in three engine sizes. The aluminum tunnel was stretched out to accept a lengthened, C-7 suspension system with a deep profile, 15x136in track. Overall length of the machine was 118in. To improve maneuverability in deep snow, the ski stance was narrowed from the Formula's 40in to 36in. Wide plastic skis improved flotation and reduced drag in sticky snow conditions. The Summit was originally produced with 467 and 583 type engines. Demand from the very high altitude areas spurred the late production of the 670 Summit.

The Summit was designed as a deep powder machine, which automatically associated it with the mountainous areas. Varying altitudes change the fuel-air mixture delivered to the engine and a system to automatically compensate for the altitude changes could be a real boon to the mountain rider. EFI systems can handle the adjustment automatically but the systems are expensive and heavy. Bombardier-Rotax had been developing a device to do the job using slightly modified carburetors and a device they called a High Altitude Compensator (HAC).

A chamber in the HAC is filled with a reference pressure and sealed with a diaphragm that controls the position of a double ended needle. The chamber of the HAC is mounted in the air silencer box where it can sense the temperature and the ambient pressure. The needle valve moves in or out based on the ambient conditions vs the reference pressure. The needle valves control air between atmospheric pressure and the lowest pressure present in the venturi of the carburetors. A line connects the adjusted pressure from the HAC to the unvented float bowls of the carburetor. An increase in the pressure in the float bowl results in the fuel mixture becoming richer; while a decrease the pressure in the float bowl causes the mixture to lean out. The clever, lightweight system was standard equipment on all Summit models.

The Summits were built with a single-passenger seat and no rear rack. Heated hand grips and thumb warmers were standard on all the Summits as was the dark green metallic finish on the hoods. A high windshield, speedometer, and tachometer were also standard equipment.

Bombardier's two millionth Ski-Doo was produced in late August of 1993. The machine on the assembly line at the time was the 1994 Summit 583. It seemed fitting that the Summit 583, as the two millionth Ski-Doo, would be joining a 1974 T'NT Everest 440, the one millionth Ski-Doo, in the J-Armand Bombardier Museum.

1995

(Some details are missing at the time of this writing. Not all specifications have been released.)

The success of the F-2000, all-aluminum chassis has been so great that all but three models in Ski-Doo's line-up are built on what started as the new Formula chassis. Only the legendary Élan, the twin-track Alpine II, and the Finnish-built Scandic Wide Track are produced on other chassis designs.

Even a Scandic, sport-utility sled is spun off on the new chassis. Available with a type 503 or a type 377 fan-cooled engine, both models run a 15x136in track and wide, steel skis. Reverse gear, cargo racks, and high windshields are standard equipment. At the rear is Ski-Doo's new suspension with 10in of vertical travel.

Ski-Doo's 1995 Formula Z features the durable and powerful 583 RAVE-valved Rotax engine, H.P.G. shocks, the F-2000 chassis, and hydraulic brakes. *Bombardier Corp.*

While the Mach Z, MX Z, and Summit returned on the new chassis, many other models benefited from the new design for 1995. The Mach I now rode on the F-2000 chassis as did the all new Formula SL and Formula S (shown here), economical sport performance models. *Bombardier Corp.*

The Summit 470 is dropped from the line and the Summit 670 becomes a full production model along with the 583. The 670 is fitted with a new track with 1.25in-long traction lugs set in an alternating, angled fashion across the track.

Six models of touring sleds are built on the F-2000 chassis. Liquid-cooled 670, 582, and 467 engines are available on C-7 suspensions with 7.5in of travel. The fan-cooled engines include the 503 and 377. The 503 has standard electric start and an electric start version of the 377 is available. The three air-cooled touring models all ride on the new, long-travel, twin-shock suspension system offering 10in of vertical travel. Reverse gear is standard on all models except the L and LE, which are powered by the 377 engine. All touring models run a 15x136in track. A blue hood is used on the liquid-cooled models while the air coolers were fitted with green hoods.

The MX was fitted with a type 467cc engine again and received few changes for 1995. The MX Z became the all-out cross country race sled and conformed to the rules which required a 440cc or smaller engine. The type 454 returns! You have to go back to the 1982 Blizzard 9500 to find the last use of this engine on a Ski-Doo. The engine for 1995 was vastly updated with RAVE valves, nikasil-plated cylinders with triple exhaust ports, twelve-pole magneto, single tuned exhaust system, and VM 34 carburetors. The 1982 version ran 36mm carbs but new racing rules (for 1994-1995) required no larger than 34s. The type 454 engine displaced 436.6cc with its 67.5mm bores and 61mm stroke and fit neatly into the new displacement rule.

The engine was lowered in the chassis for 1995 and HPG, rebuildable shocks were used all around on the MX Z. The adjustable stabilizer bar was retained from the previous season. A narrow steel ski was used on the MX Z while the MX was fitted with wide steel skis. Both MXs used the triple shock, C-7 rear suspension. A hydraulic brake was standard on the MX Z only.

The Mach I and Mach Z maintained their black colors for 1995 and shared the same all aluminum chassis with HPG (High Pressure Gas) shocks all the way around. The only significant difference between the sleds is the engine. The Mach I again ran the type 670 twin but this time with twin tuned pipes and 44mm carbs while the Mach Z got the updated 779 triple. Both sleds had a 15x121in track, and hydraulic brakes are standard on both Machs.

The Formula name returned in numbers for 1995 with five separate models, all finished in red. The Formula SL was the first Formula to use an air-cooled engine, the venerable 503 with twin, 34mm carbs and a single tuned pipe. Only the SL used the new, 10in long-travel suspension, while all others rode on the improved C-7 design.

The Formula STX was produced in a long track version, the Formula STX LT with a 15x136in track. Both were powered by the RAVE-valved type 583 engine with

The 1995 Grand Touring models rode on the new chassis and offered many new features. *Bombardier Corp.*

38mm carbs. HPG shocks were used at the rear arm of the STXs.

If you were looking for a street rod, the 1995 Formula SS was it. It was powered by the type 670 engine as used in the 1994 Mach I. Only 44mm carbs and twin tuned pipes separate its power output from the 1995 Mach I's. The Formula SS was equipped with a single expansion chamber and dual, VM 40 Mikunis. Still boast-

Even the sport-utility class Skandic got the plush ride of the F-2000 chassis for 1995. *Bombardier Corp.*

ing a lot of features like carbide runners, handlebar and thumb warmers, wide steel skis, speedometer, and tachometer, the Formula SS was a bare bones hot rod.

The Formula Z was the top of the new Formula line and was set up with competition in mind. The 583 engine was equipped with 40mm carbs, and hydraulic brakes were standard equipment, as was an adjustable sway bar. HPG shocks mounted on the ski suspension and the rear arm, and plastic skis with carbide runners added to top speed and control.

Thirty-six years of Ski-Doo have created an industry and a sport, revitalized the winter economy in many use areas, opened the once frozen north for people to work and recreate in, and provided millions of hours of just plain fun. I am so thankful Joseph-Armand Bombardier wasn't born and raised in Florida!

1995 Models on the F-2000 Chassis

	Scandic 380	Scandic 500	Touring L/LE
Overall length	113.6in	113.6in	106.1/113.6in
Overall widthin	42.5in	42.5in	42.5in
Approx. weight	433lb	455lb	418/437lb
Ski stance	37in	37in	40in
Fuel capacity	10.6 US gal	10.6 US gal	10.6 US gal
Track width	15in	15in	15in
Track length	136in	136in	121in
Bore	62mm	72mm	62mm
Stroke	61mm	61mm	61mm
Displacement	368.3cc	496.7cc	368.3cc
Carburetor	2 VM 30	2 VM 34	2 VM 30

	Touring SLE	GT 470/580	GT SE 670
Overall length	113.6in	114.6/118.9in	118.9in
Overall width	45.5in	45.5in	45.5in
Approx. weight	468lb	514/550lb	555lb
Ski stance	40in	40in	40in
Fuel capacity	10.6 US gal	11.1 US gal	11.1 US gal
Track width	15in	15in	15in
Track length	136in	136in	136in
Bore	72mm	69.5/76mm	78mm
Stroke	61mm	61/64mm	70mm
Displacement	496.7cc	462.2/58.7cc	669cc
Carburetor	2 VM 34	2-34/2-38	2 VM 40

	Summit 583/670	MX/MX Z
Overall length	114.6in	107.1in
Overall width	42.5in	45.5/44.5in
Approx. weight	513/521lb	485/477lb
Ski stance	37in	40in
Fuel capacity	11.1 US gal	11.1/9.8 US gal
Track width	15in	15in
Track length	136in	121in
Bore	76/78mm	69.5/67.7mm
Stroke	64/70mm	61mm
Displacement	580.7/669cc	462.8/436.6cc
Carburetor	2 VM 38/2 VM 40	2 VM 34

	Formula SL	Formula STX/LT
Overall length	106.1in	107.1/114.6in
Overall width	45.5in	45.5in
Approx. weight	424lb	504/513lb
Ski stance	40in	40in
Fuel capacity	10.6 US gal	11.1 US gal
Track width	15in	15in
Track length	121in	121/136in
Bore	72mm	76mm
Stroke	61mm	64mm
Displacement	496.7cc	580.7cc
Carburetor	2 VM 34	2 VM 38

	Form SS	Form Z	Mach I	Mach Z
Overall length	107.1in	107.1in	107.1in	107.1in
Overall width	45.5in	45.5in	45.5in	45.5in
Approx. weight	527lb	502lb	529lb	533lb
Ski stance	40in	40in	40in	40in
Fuel capacity	11.1 US	11.1 US	11.1 US	11.1 US gal
Track width	15in	15in	15in	15in
Track length	121in	121in	121in	121in
Bore	78mm	76mm	78mm	69.5mm
Stroke	70mm	64mm	70mm	68mm
Displacement	669cc	580.7cc	669cc	773.9cc
Carburetor	2 VM 40	2 VM 40	2 VM 44	3-TM 38

Index